Successful Sports Officiating

Jerry Grunska, Editor

Referee *Magazine*

*National Association
of Sports Officials*

Human Kinetics

Library of Congress Cataloging-in-Publication Data

Successful sports officiating / edited by Jerry Grunska for Referee magazine.

           p.   m.

          Includes index.

          ISBN 0-88011-748-6

          1. Sports officiating.   I. Grunska, Jerry.   II. Referee (Franksville, Wis.)

       GV735.S93   1999

       796--dc21   99-30329

                                                                     CIP

ISBN-10: 0-88011-748-6
ISBN-13: 978-0-88011-748-7

Acquisitions Editor: Tom Hanlon
Developmental Editors: Joanna G. Hatzopoulos and Sydney Slobodnik
Assistant Editor: John Wentworth
Copyeditor: Karen Bojda
Proofreader: Jim Burns
Indexer: Gerry Lynn Messner
Graphic Designer: Robert Reuther
Illustrators: Theo Cobb and Andrew Sestak
Graphic Artist: Judy Henderson
Photo Editors: Jeff Stern and Clark Brooks
Cover Photographer: Tom Roberts
Interior photographers: Photographs provided by Human Kinetics, Referee, and IHSA; individual photographers listed with photographs, except: page 85, ©Dale Garvey; pages 39 and 115, ©Jeff Soucek/IHSA; and pages iv–v, 1, and 143, ©Human Kinetics.
Cover Designer: Jack W. Davis
Printer: United Graphics

Printed in the United States of America   10 9 8 7

Human Kinetics
Web site: www.HumanKinetics.com

United States: Human Kinetics
P.O. Box 5076
Champaign, IL 61825-5076
800-747-4457
e-mail: humank@hkusa.com

Canada: Human Kinetics
475 Devonshire Road, Unit 100
Windsor, ON N8Y 2L5
800-465-7301 (in Canada only)
e-mail: info@hkcanada.com

Europe: Human Kinetics
107 Bradford Road
Stanningley
Leeds LS28 6AT, United Kingdom
+44 (0)113 255 5665
e-mail: hk@hkeurope.com

Australia: Human Kinetics
57A Price Avenue
Lower Mitcham, South Australia 5062
08 8372 0999
e-mail: info@hkaustralia.com

New Zealand: Human Kinetics
Division of Sports Distributors NZ Ltd.
P.O. Box 300 226 Albany
North Shore City, Auckland
0064 9 448 1207
e-mail: info@humankinetics.co.nz

Successful Sports Officiating

Contents

Acknowledgments

Special recognition goes to the following individuals who have so generously contributed their efforts and creativity to the final product: Jerry Grunska, for decades a highly respected football official, who served as the book's editor; Bob Messina, Travis Doster, Brian Spurlock, Boothe Davis, John De Freitas, and Dale Garvey for providing us with so many insightful photographs; and Jeff Stern and Lisa Martin of *Referee* magazine, who served as our graphics resource experts.

—Barry Mano

I wish to thank the experts who contributed to this text. Each of them worked hard to fulfill the goals of the project. Each writer drew upon a specialist's background to develop the respective chapters: Attorney Mel Narol, instructors and therapists Drs. Jon and Kathleen Poole, freelance writer Kay Roof-Steffen, motivational counselor Dr. George Selleck, editor of *Referee* Bill Topp, health administrator Doug Toole, and Ohio state High School Athletic Association Assistant Commissioner Henry Zaborniak, Jr. I also wish to thank Barry Mano for having the vision to create the initial concept of this book; he helped it become a reality.

—Jerry Grunska

© Paul Willette

Foreword

Sports officiating is rewarding but also challenging. The common image of an official standing his or her ground while being yelled at by a player, coach, or fan can and does happen to every official, but your overall experience as an official will be exhilarating and positive and will more than compensate for the occasional verbal abuse you'll encounter. The skills you develop as an official will serve you throughout your life.

To be a good official, you need a blend of many qualities, including courage, self-confidence, determination, and decisiveness. In each game that you work, you will be faced with many problems; to solve them all you will be asked to demonstrate the fairness of a judge, the skill of a diplomat, the authority of a police officer, and the understanding of a parent. All in all, much will be asked of you.

If officials have people yelling at them and have to make quick decisions and get sweaty doing it, why in the world would anyone want to officiate? The answer is easy. People officiate to give back to the game and because they believe sports are a valuable component of education. They officiate because they want the challenge of keeping order and ensuring fairness when chaos lurks at every turn of events. They officiate because they relish the opportunity to undertake a tough assignment and succeed at it. When the game is done and you know you have done a proper and fair job, you will have a special feeling of accomplishment, even though there might still be boos ringing in your ears. Learning to live with the boos is just one more ingredient of becoming a good official.

Learning to be a good official has never been easy. When I began refereeing basketball in 1960, we learned the craft by listening to veteran officials and by working as many scrimmages and games as we could. Other than the rule and case books, the main reference publication was a book written in 1950 by John Bunn, *The Art of Officiating Sport.*

The world has certainly changed since Bunn's time. Those who play and coach sports today have vastly different perspectives and expectations than they did in 1950. To be an effective and well-accepted official today, you need to understand the entire sports experience, that sports are "life with the volume turned up." That understanding provides the basis for developing your personal philosophy of officiating. In addition to this philosophy, you need to study, absorb, and turn into action the training materials that give you a proper base of knowledge.

What does a sport official need to know? The easy answer is the rules and proper positioning and mechanics. Those two bodies of knowledge are critically important to any official. To succeed today, though, you need to know more. For example, you'll need to have a basic understanding of your legal rights and responsibilities, proper nutrition and conditioning, time management, the techniques of game management, and how to develop and maximize a personal officiating style.

Until now there wasn't a single source of this vital information. *Successful Sports Officiating* fills that void. It is the most comprehensive and authoritative text on the subject that has ever been published. I know that you will find within its pages answers to the questions that you ask yourself about becoming and succeeding as an official. The book has been written and edited by a team of expert practitioners of the art and science of officiating. Their hands-on experience and practical approach will serve you well in your quest to understand and apply the basic principles of successful officiating. You'll be able to apply the principles, practices, and policies from this book in each game that you work.

—Barry Mano

President, National Association of Sport Officials
Publisher, Referee Magazine

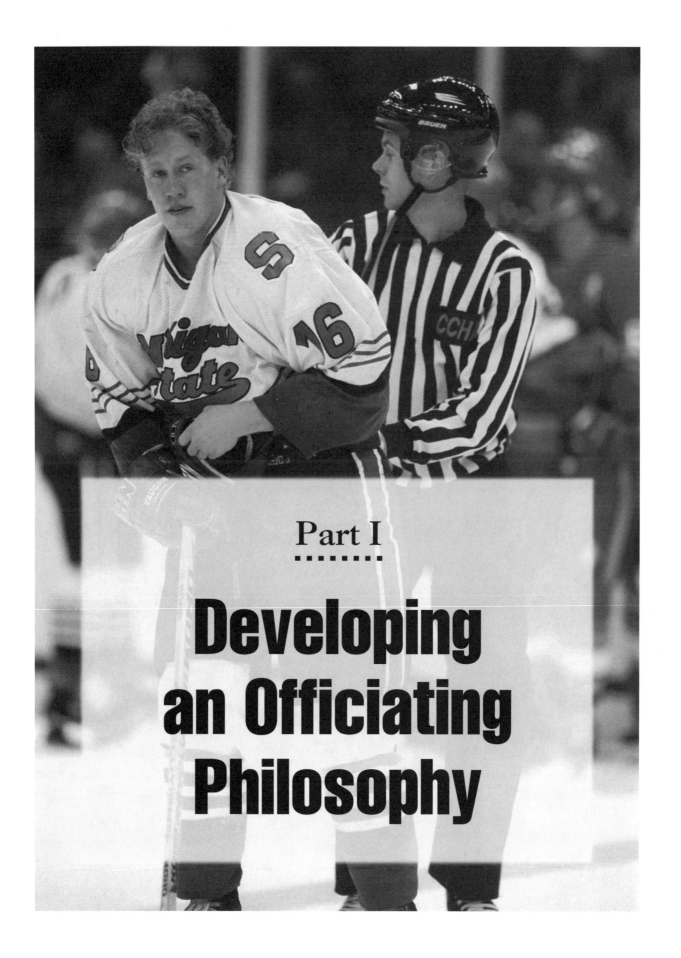

Part I
....

Developing
an Officiating
Philosophy

1

Your Officiating Objectives

Jerry Grunska

In this chapter you'll learn

■ four essential objectives of officiating,

■ five reasons people work hard to be good officials, and

■ appropriate ethics for officials.

This chapter explores some of the main reasons why sports officiating can be a useful and satisfying vocation or avocation. The objectives that help to shape an official's role are introduced.

Basically, officials help people play games. Officials' responsibilities include making sure that principles of fairness are observed, that games take place in a manner that ensures the safety of participants, that players employ positive elements of sportsmanship, and that the people playing have a chance to develop their skills and knowledge of the sport.

With an investment of time and effort, a sports official can derive satisfaction from helping players achieve the preceding goals; in addition, an official can continue an association with sports while building a career that can furnish supplemental income. For the most enjoyment and to gain the best reputation, an official must continually demonstrate strong ethical behavior.

Essential Objectives

Officials' primary responsibilities are ensuring the safety of players, making sure that games are played fairly according to the rules, helping players develop their skills and knowledge of their sport, and promoting sportsmanship.

Enhancing Game Safety

Officials are responsible for the physical well-being of players in a variety of ways. One way that officials enhance players' safety is by ensuring that players are properly equipped. Officials inspect and approve game equipment (such as hockey sticks, field hockey wickets, baseball and softball bats, and football measuring devices). They inspect the facilities, including the playing surface and surrounding area, to be sure that dangers are identified and eliminated if possible. Officials enforce the contest rules that have been designed to protect players and make certain that injuries are attended to in a proper manner. Finally, although an official's jurisdiction may not extend to control of spectators, at times an official may find it necessary to protect a participant from threats of harm by opponents or onlookers.

Inspecting Protective Equipment

The rules provide for an inspection of player equipment for several reasons. Equipment rules are based on broad historical experience, and equipment specifications are drawn so as to provide maximum player protection. For example, precise specifications for the protective helmets that participants wear in several sports (such as hockey, field hockey, baseball, and football) are described in the rules, and in some cases an approved seal must be attached to the helmet to certify its legality. In addition, a variety of protective padding for the shoulders, face, limbs, hands, ribs, tailbone, thighs, and knees may also be spelled out in the rules. In some sports, mouthpieces must be worn, and shoe cleats of a certain size and type are permitted. The cleats are restricted in composition and length so as to present the least danger to the wearer and to opponents. The rules also often specify what cannot be worn. In some cases, casts that cover injured bones are allowed, but they must be padded with a precise thickness of "slow recovery" material. In sports where physical contact and kicking are part of the action, hard leather shoes or hiking boots are not permitted.

Officials must inspect player equipment to be sure it complies with the rules. For example, football players who play positions in which speed and agility are essential often remove their hip, tail, and thigh pads to reduce what they consider unnecessary weight from their uniforms. (These padding devices, which have a hard outer shell against outside forces and a soft inner layer against the skin, usually fit into pockets in the uniform and are easily removed.) The rules of a sport describe what equipment must be worn, what is optional, what may be removed, and how it must be replaced if it is torn or broken.

A regular procedure for officials to check player equipment is spelled out in the rules and mechanics manuals. In practice, the procedure may be abbreviated or circumvented by the coach certifying verbally that players are properly equipped, though it is often impractical for a coach to observe the way all team members put on their uniforms. Therefore, wise officials spot-check players during warm-ups or pregame drills, or even in the dressing room before a game. Neglect of this duty could result in severe consequences for the officials if it were discovered later that an injury was caused by improper player equipment, such as protective padding deliberately altered or removed or faulty equipment that became defective through game action.

Inspecting Game Equipment

There are exact specifications in the rules for equipment used in games, and officials must know what those "specs" are and what to do about nonstandard equipment. For example, softball players may not use baseball ("hardball") bats, and a baseball bat may have tape only a certain distance up the handle from the gripping knob. No screws are permitted to secure a bat that may be cracked. Umpires are issued little circular cards that slip over the barrel of a bat to verify its legality. In football, the stakes at the ends of the measuring chain must be blunt and rounded; they cannot have a sharp point. Lines on the field must be of a nontoxic material. In the past, lime was often used to mark boundary lines, and it frequently burned players when it got in their eyes or in open wounds.

Officials need not inspect every item of equipment for every game. But a cursory look at such things as goals, nets, pylons, and playing implements can ensure that a game does not have to be interrupted to correct a problem discovered during the course of play. Often coaches and players notice an irregularity during pregame drills: an unanchored volleyball standard, a loose basketball net, or an underinflated soccer ball. Items needing correction can be brought to the officials' attention, and adjustments can be accomplished.

Inspecting Facilities

A game most often takes place where many games have gone on before, but that does not necessarily mean that facilities are free of hazards. For example, outdoor games are frequently held inside the oval of a track, which may have curbs, vaulting pits, concrete runways, and such. Usually these are far enough off the playing field to pose no problems. Through faulty design, however, some permanent objects such as concrete barricades or stationary benches are too close to the field. Players may charge into them under their own momentum or be forced into them by opponents. When officials discover hazards, such as above-ground water spigots or scuffed turf due to previous activity on the field, they should call them to the attention of the game management.

In cases where padding or covering with other material would suffice, such protections should be requested.

Indoor hazards can be equally dangerous. Water fountains too close to the court, gymnastic equipment not removed, ropes hanging obtrusively, or faulty flooring (such as floors that are overwaxed or have a residue of dust or water melting from boots in the winter) can all pose problems. These hazards may not have been present in previous contests on that same floor. The fountain would have been there, of course, but if the prior activity was a wrestling match, the fountain's proximity was immaterial. Facility hazards must be the concern of officials, and wherever possible, officials should request protective or corrective measures before allowing a game to begin. Simply placing an exercise mat across the

Never forget that you're "on stage." If you let your guard down, people might take advantage and besmirch your image. This official may have been ill, but no one will ever know that. The scene does not reveal whatever discomfort he may have had. He just chose to recline at an unfortunate time.

base of a volleyball standard, for example, may be all that is needed to prevent player injury.

Regulating Game Conduct

The rules of a sport specify which kinds of player contact are legitimate and which are forbidden. It is up to the official to know these rules thoroughly and to enforce penalties when a player's behavior violates those provisions. An official must also understand when an action is close to violating a rule and may be dangerous. In such cases, the official must learn when to issue a warning and when to penalize the act without a warning. An official must also recognize when perfectly legal acts may cause tempers to flare. All of these situations require an official to make fine distinctions in judging play action in order to guard player safety. Officials' legal responsibilities are the topic of chapter 10.

Mean-spirited attitudes may also jeopardize player safety. Officials must be able to recognize belligerence and have a strategy for dealing with it. Animosities have a tendency to escalate if they are not addressed in a meaningful way early in a contest. Strategies for dealing with conflict are introduced in chapter 6.

Injury Response

Most sports nowadays have a "flowing blood" rule whereby an injured participant must leave the game and be attended to before being allowed to continue playing. Open wounds that have resulted from game action or abrasions and lacerations previously acquired but newly reopened need to be cleaned and covered. Blood-soaked uniforms need to be replaced. The reason for the rule is that disease can be spread via contact with blood from a wound.

It may seem a simple matter for an official to observe blood flowing from a wound. But in games featuring swift action and many players, it is possible for rather severe contusions to go unnoticed, particularly if players take steps to keep injuries hidden. Players sometimes hide injuries as a matter of pride and determination to show stamina under duress. It behooves officials to keep an eye out for excessive bleeding and for other injuries, such as wrenched limbs, reactions to head blows, and symptoms of back pain. In the case of excessive bleeding, an official must

exercise careful judgment and avoid overzealousness about minor scratches. The critical factor should be the definite possibility that blood may be transferred to another participant. An official must also distinguish between minor aches and bruises that may be a customary part of the game and major injuries, those which could hurt bones or internal organs and which may be debilitating. When in doubt about an injury, the official should make a decision on the side of caution. It is a good tactic to consult with a fellow official, a trainer, or another team representative before sending a player from the game.

When a player is on the ground or the floor because of an injury, officials should permit team attendants to work on the player. Often teams have skilled trainers or even medical personnel on hand to examine and treat players' injuries. The officials' job is to allow careful examination and not to rush any player off the premises, particularly if a head, neck, or back injury is evident. Officials should hold up the game for as long as necessary to remove a grounded player.

Officials should not ordinarily act as first-aid administrators in the event of player injuries, although no restrictions can be absolute. An occasion may arise where an official is the only qualified and knowledgeable person at hand, in which case proper treatment is imperative and general policies can be bypassed.

Crowd Response

Controlling crowd reaction is often not within officials' province. Game administrators are usually charged with that responsibility. Nevertheless, sometimes people from the sidelines intrude upon the arena, either by their physical presence or by unacceptable behavior, and then officials are obliged to become involved.

If spectators are close by, say in a small gym in folding chairs near the court, and an unruly individual or group begins to berate players or officials in an unacceptable way, officials should ask game administrators to remove the people who are causing the disturbance. Rarely should officials engage the audience directly. If no game administrator is present, officials may have to call on coaches to quell unruly onlookers.

If a member of the audience moves onto the playing surface to attack a player, officials should intercept that person or group and should make sure that the playing area is free of all threats before continuing the game.

Unfortunately, in today's society and in the sports milieu, propriety sometimes gives way to unseemly and even violent behavior, and officials may find themselves caught in the middle, even as targets of abuse. Officials should respond to threats from spectators as much as they are able by protecting the players. If a regrettable incident takes place, officials should try to identify witnesses and report the happenings to the proper authorities so that legal action can be accurately pursued.

Striving for Fairness

Sometimes officials have to make decisions about nearly every act in a team game. At other times athletic contests require only a minimum of officiating interference. In some ways officials act as aids to the action, and in others they must make continual judgments about the acts that constitute the basic elements of the sport. Making these decisions requires two traits: a full understanding of what is supposed to take place in a game and a superior ability to make distinctions about those factors. The fundamental purpose of offi-

cials is to make sure that games proceed in a fair manner.

It is possible to mistake this purpose. Some officials feel it is their primary duty to call violations, to punish participants whenever possible, to conduct a kind of competition themselves to see how much influence they can have on the proceedings. But the real purpose of officials is to help players play a game.

It may seem obvious that an official must be fair, but sometimes this doctrine is hard to maintain. If a friend or relative is playing, the official may lean in that team's direction without realizing it. If one team "chips" at the official from the start of the game, whereas the other squad doesn't utter a word of complaint, it will be difficult to keep a balanced view of the action. If just one player on a team voices sarcasm, remaining entirely neutral becomes problematic. But the official's task is to subdue his or her emotions and make an honest call when a key play occurs.

Sometimes an official will go to a game with disturbing things in mind: a residue of anger from a previous experience with a team, a quarrel at home, a confrontation at work, a disappointment in a project, an auto mishap on the way to the game. In addition to affecting one's concentration, such an emotional state can influence

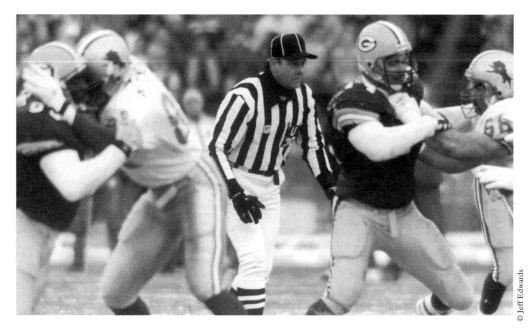

© Jeff Edwards

Officials such as Dennis Riggs talk to players, observe their actions during breaks in play, and use preventive officiating techniques, which are often more effective than meting out punishment.

As sports programs continue to grow, officiating opportunities increase as well. Youth games are a great starting point for any official breaking into the avocation.

© Referee

attempts to be neutral in dealing with teams during the game.

Officials must learn how strictly rules must be applied at various levels of competition. It is possible to ruin the game by applying all technical aspects of the rules. If the game is a high school junior varsity game, rules may be applied differently than they would in a varsity game. This can be called the advantage/disadvantage principle.

As an example, at the high school underclass level in baseball, a player-coach may step into the baseline to extend a pat on the back as a teammate rounds third base and heads for home plate. At a higher level, this contact would result in the runner's being called out. At the subvarsity level, though, a soft reminder may be all that's needed, as no advantage was gained by the act. Similarly, an official would permit junior varsity basketball players on both teams a slight shuffle of the feet when trying to pivot because, once again, no advantage has been gained. Strict adherence to rules governing all individual maneuvers might result in a continual blowing of the whistle and can actually take the game away from the players.

In essence, fairness can be defined as a solid knowledge of the rules applied in an even way to game action. The rules are designed so that one team does not enjoy an unfair advantage. Fairness in administering a game can extend beyond the immediate game surface and also beyond the basic rules of play. For example, officials have had to muffle school bands when they drown out a quarterback's signal calling.

Aiding in Athletes' Development

Officials are not coaches, and they risk criticism when they try to act like coaches. Nevertheless, at times officials can help players better understand a game and improve their skills. There are rule situations, for example, that an official can explain. A basketball official may notify a player that she can "run" the baseline when trying to pass in bounds after a basket is made. Baseball and softball players can be told the consequences of stepping out of the batter's box, of running out of the baseline, and of interfering with fielders. Football players can be reminded that they must not interfere with a quarterback's signal calling, that they cannot cross the sideline during a live ball, and that a false snap does not put the ball in play. In other words, officials can inform players about rules that players seldom see enforced and about which their coaches may not have alerted them. Few coaches have thorough knowledge about rare rule applications.

It is pushing the limits of protocol, however, to tell a baseball or softball runner that he could have tagged up and advanced on a caught foul fly, that she could have reached into out-of-play territory to catch a ball in flight, or that he was not automatically out when the catcher dropped a third strike, but an official must judge what is appropriate according to the level of play and what is customary according to league or state policy.

Sometimes, in sports where contact is either permissible or unavoidable, an official can help a

Official and Teacher

Following are two examples of how an official can help players develop.

• Umpire Larry Campbell of Elizabethtown, Kentucky, said he helped high school pitcher Sean Bennett with proper footwork when Bennett was learning to pitch at the junior varsity level. "It was either give him a few hints or call him for balking," Campbell said. "I told him that he had to take his sign while his back foot was on the rubber and that he had to step to first to make a throw. I caught him between innings as he was coming off the diamond, and I asked the coach to listen. Both were appreciative." Campbell later watched as Bennett became a strong varsity pitcher.

• Basketball official John Katzler of Mt. Prospect, Illinois, often speaks to high school teams and offers demonstrations by way of preseason orientation. "I get a dribbler out there on the floor, and I have him race downcourt, stop, and then pivot while still dribbling. Then I can show what is a 'carry' and what is not," Katzler said. Katzler also shows what constitutes legal and illegal contact on blocked shots, on screens, and in a double-team pressing defense. "The whole idea is to alert them to what is proper and what things to practice on to improve their skills," said Katzler.

player understand that certain acts are forbidden, such as leaping over an opponent to intercept a pass or undercutting a basketball player trying a lay-up. By cautioning players, an official may actually change participants' behavior, improve their skills, and increase their knowledge of the sport they are playing.

It is acceptable under some conditions to notify players if they are about to commit a violation or to help them line up. In basketball, if a player's foot is on the lane line before a ball is handed to a free-throw shooter, it is not only sensible, it is practically mandatory that the players be told to watch their feet. Football officials ordinarily help high school players line up on the scrimmage line, especially if field markings are faint. A plate umpire in baseball or softball invariably warns a batter if the batter's box is close to being violated. Warnings and official hints like these vary from sport to sport, and the official must learn exactly what is feasible and what is forbidden. Although not a primary goal, helping players play can be a useful officiating objective.

Promoting Sportsmanship

Any time an official can positively reinforce a gracious act, the game and the performers receive a genuine service. In some sports, for example, after learning what is acceptable, an official can feel free to compliment players when they make outstanding plays. At the high school level, there is nothing wrong with a baseball or softball umpire saying "nice catch" or "good hit" during a dead-ball interval or with a basketball referee or football official saying "good pass" or "great defense" if an opportunity allows. A strong illustration of teamwork, as when a player reacts in a manner that clearly helps achieve a group goal, can be acknowledged, or a player avoiding a violation can be commended. Naturally, such comments should be judiciously offered in a low key manner directly to the participant during breaks in action so that no spectator is likely to observe the exchange. One must take pains not to be obvious about this; an official is not at liberty to be a cheerleader.

The best way an official can influence players' behavior is to acknowledge acts of sportsmanship. A softball player picks up the catcher's mask and hands it over after the catcher has chased a foul ball; a third baseman helps a runner brush dust off a uniform after a slide; a basketball player picks up an opponent after a collision; a football player twists aside to avoid an unnecessary hit on a runner; all of these acts and many more can be applauded verbally by officials. The official need not make a show of the acknowledgment, but subtle assertions can work positively at times in promoting wholesome competition. For the most part, players prefer to respect their opponents.

Officials should keep in mind that sometimes good sportsmanship runs counter to what players are taught and is in contrast to the atmosphere of the game. Yet players usually feel more comfortable and get genuine satisfaction from acting in a noble way. A timely remark from an official can actually have more influence under certain circumstances than a combative coach or adversarial onlookers.

Personal Objectives

There are many personal benefits to be gained from sports officiating. Many officials enjoy being part of the intense action of sports and find fulfillment in using their skills to help players improve and compete fairly. Officiating often involves enjoyable interaction with others, from athletes to groundskeepers. Some officials seek the opportunity to continue participation in a sport or to remain physically active. Officiating can even be a profitable part-time career.

Intensity and Focus

NFL quarterback Jake Plummer of the Arizona Cardinals explained his calmness in the middle of game turmoil. "It's so high energy. Yet everything is narrowed toward one goal and your focus goes toward that. . . . I don't hear the crowd. It's like whatever senses don't need to be turned on just turn off."[1]

Plummer was describing the actions of participants, of course, but his description could also apply to officials. Officials can get caught up in a game as determinedly as players, catching the fever of strong intensity, ignoring the crowd, giving in to a focus that is aimed entirely at the immediate objective, namely, to see with keen perception, to record discrete images of events in the mind, and to make sharp judgments about what is fair and what is not. Achieving a high level of skill and efficiency can even be called artistic.

A beginning official cannot accomplish this just by walking onto a field or court and calling a game "cold." This misconception about officiating can

---

[1]Michael Silver, "More Than Meets The Eye," *Sports Illustrated*, 17 August 1998, 75.

Despite what you may hear in the stands or on the sidelines, officiating decisions require knowledge, practice, and courage.

be compared to a person watching an auto race and saying, "I know how to drive a car. I could do that." To race successfully takes a considerable amount of practice, skill, and courage. Although spectators and players often feel free to question the accuracy of officiating decisions, to make those decisions during games requires intricate knowledge, much practice in putting that knowledge to work, and, yes, a generous supply of courage.

Personal Interactions

Sports officiating at any level offers the opportunity to meet many people. The players themselves may take officials for granted initially, but if officials work for the same players more than once, before long the players become friendly. They may chat about things related to the game during lulls in the action, drawing the officials into the game and making them feel a part of it.

Officials meet a host of people connected to the sport: coaches, game administrators, concessionaires, scorekeepers, timers, parking supervisors, band directors, groundskeepers, assignors, and, most important of all, fellow officials. Other officials serve an important role, helping newcomers feel comfortable working games and increasing their understanding of how to work properly. Officiating companions may be the readiest source of learning.

Another satisfaction is the feeling of helping people to perform at their best. While players try to exercise their skills at playing the game, officials ensure that players' actions will be judged fairly and that the rules will be upheld. People don't always compliment officials, though. Maybe another official will shake hands after a game, but that may be the extent of appreciation expressed. The pleasure of doing the job well may have to come from inside an official's own heart and mind.

Continued Association With a Sport

Another enticing factor about officiating is that anyone can join. There are virtually no age restrictions. Although prep sports are likely to be handled exclusively by adults, many municipal organizations recruit, train, and employ teenagers for the youth programs in all sports. Advanced

age is no barrier either. Retirees over 60 have been welcomed into softball as umpires, and some of them work several hundred games a year. Almost no one is turned away who expresses eagerness, including people with impaired mobility.

> Jack McKenna, 67, an umpire from Lakewood, Colorado, just reported working 623 softball games from March to November: doubleheaders five nights a week and eight games a day in weekend tournaments.
>
> A 95-year-old soccer referee, Harry Rodgers from Boca Raton, Florida, worked 26 high school games in 1998. He has officiated 4,301 games in a 71-year career.[2]

Sometimes people turn to officiating to prolong their athletic involvement. It is not necessary to be a former athlete, although that is sometimes the case, but it does help to have a working knowledge of the sport. Officiating is like playing in that, to officiate well, one has to anticipate players' actions as if one were operating as a performer. Without a knowledge of the game, it will take longer to become an effective official. Neophytes are frequently caught out of position, maybe even staring at the wrong thing, unable to make an accurate ruling. Knowing the game reduces surprises. Officiating is unlike playing, on the other hand, because the official does not have to make the plays. No actual game skills are required.

Physical Activity

Depending on the sport, physical activity for an official can be mild, moderate, or vigorous. A volleyball official just has to stand on a ladder and wave her arms, whereas a basketball official must move nearly as fast as the players and must run what amounts to a marathon each outing. It has been estimated that soccer officials, for instance, undertake between five and six miles of steady exertion per match, and basketball officials cover three miles in an underclass game and four in a varsity contest.

A baseball umpire may not run as much, but covering the game can require squatting and rising from a crouch 500 times a game plus occasional short dashes to follow balls hit into the

---

[2]"For the Record," *Referee*, September 1998, 74.

Not every sport has demanding physical requirements, but many, including basketball, soccer, and hockey (superior skating skills necessary!) depend on officials being in outstanding condition.

outfield and to cover bases where plays are being made. Football officials get about 20 seconds of recovery time for every 5- to l0-yard dash to cover game action. For some people, just standing through a lengthy game could be a chore.

Officiating can provide an individual with consistent, enjoyable physical activity, but it would be misleading for a person to feel that working games can serve as physical conditioning. The conditioning should take place before the games begin. That is what athletes do: get ready to play before they compete. Athletes are generally much younger and in peak condition when they play. Officials can't hope to keep up with the players if they have not made an effort to be in sound condition. However, working games in the season on a regular basis can help sustain physical conditioning: expanded lung capacity, healthy heart and metabolic rates, and muscle suppleness.

Building a Small Business

One dimension of officiating sports, of course, is that it can become a part-time job; stipends are paid, and sometimes even travel allowances are part of a game fee. The pay scales vary for different sports, different levels, and different regions from year to year. Some officials consider officiating a serious second career; often they are also interested in advancing to higher levels, aiming for college assignments and perhaps even professional sports.

The official is considered an independent contractor. The legal implications of this are discussed in chapters 9 and 10. Chapter 10 also outlines some business practices for independent contractors that officials should know about.

Officiating becomes a beneficial part-time career for many individuals. In some sports, games are scheduled so frequently that an ambitious person can work nearly every day. Also, some officials use their versatility by working several sports at a time. Some high school officials are content to work a single game or a doubleheader on weekends; others hustle to work as many games as possible. But take care not to let your officiating suffer just to fit more games into your schedule. The official who works primarily for the compensation and does not really care about the games or the athletes, who is instead bent on finishing games quickly and moving on to the next venue, is scorned by those who are committed to professionalism.

The Official's Ethics

Sports officials must embrace the four essential objectives discussed at the beginning of this chapter: ensuring player safety, administering games fairly, helping athletes develop, and promoting all-around sportsmanship. Beyond these issues, another key element is for officials to embody integrity. Despite much cynicism about political, economic, and personal interactions, people place

© Theo Cobb

"That pitch was at least an inch and a half inside." Criticism from coaches, players, spectators, and the media are part of the officiating territory. Because most often those making the comments have a rooting interest in one of the teams and rarely have little more than a working knowledge of rules and mechanics, their comments are best ignored.

considerable faith in the purity of sports. Officials are charged with upholding that perception of purity.

The *appearance* of favoritism, while impossible to prove, often results in extreme distrust and vilification. Though the importance of individual games is often wildly exaggerated, players, coaches, and followers really care who wins in sports competition. Each game generates a fervent, even rabid, atmosphere. That is what makes sports so exciting, but that also means that a third party involved in the game must make courageous, objective decisions about player action—judgments that are not marred by the taint of bias.

If a person cares who wins or loses a game, he or she is taking a big chance when agreeing to officiate. Several years ago in Arizona, a strongly favored high school basketball team was on the verge of being upset in the state tournament when a controversial call permitted them to score the winning basket. It was learned after the game that the official who made that call was an administrator at the winning school. Needless to say, a series of condemnatory articles were printed in newspapers, and the official came under a barrage of criticism.

An official probably should not work games for a school he or she attended, for a school at which a spouse is employed or offspring are enrolled, nor for coaches who are close friends. But in some areas of the country, such prohibitions are impractical. Distances between towns may be too great for schools to import officials just so appearances can be maintained. But if an official has a connection to a school, it is important for the school's athletic department to be informed so that they can make an informed decision whether to use that official's services.

Showing bias toward the home team can get an official the nickname of "Homer," a derogatory term for an official who is perceived to favor the home team in calls. Stoutly ethical officials loath being thought of as favoring one team over another.

In some places officials acquire game assignments via "horse trading." For example, an athletic director at one school may officiate basketball, while his counterpart at another school is a football official. Each athletic director may save a series of games for the other, in effect, keeping outside officials from working those games. In addition, if a coach at a third school is obliged to play both schools, he or she may feel discriminated against by having to "compete" against an official as well as an opposing team. While this method of "taking care of one another" is unsavory, it nevertheless is standard practice in some quarters.

How can such unsavory practices be eliminated? There is no easy answer, because coaches and athletic directors will probably continue to have a voice in the selection of officials. But one way to minimize "you-owe-me-one" practices is to have a neutral party assign officials to games.

Another difficulty in eliminating conflicts of interest is that officials often come from the local community. A merchant who has a contract to sell goods to a school may end up officiating a contest there. A policeman who patrols the city streets may work games in his own precinct for youngsters he sees every day. Ideally, all people who officiate games would be complete strangers imported from far away, but that just isn't going to happen. In the case of sudden discoveries of conflicts of interest, not much can be done other than to notify everyone involved of the official's connection. The coach usually says, "We trust your impartiality. On with the game." If the official knows of potential difficulties in advance, he or she has an obligation to request a switch in assignments.

Summary

This opening chapter can be capsulized in the slogan: Sports officiating is serious fun. The fun comes from the exhilaration of being part of sports, in the middle of the action, expanding your own sports involvement while vigorously pursuing a profitable avocation. *Serious* suggests that being on the field or court also carries with it the obligations of protecting the players' safety, assisting in their progress as performers, ensuring that fairness is the operating principle of each contest, and promoting the noblest ideals of integrity in game conduct and in personal conduct. These may seem like esoteric ambitions, but it is each official's duty to apply them in practical working situations.

The following chapters elaborate on and develop these ideas, showing how the role of an official has many facets that need careful attention.

2

Your Officiating Style

Jerry Grunska

In this chapter you'll learn

- three styles of officiating, with reasons for their application,
- how game context affects officiating style,
- how style communicates your purposes to participants,
- personal characteristics and performance principles that lead to success, and
- the importance of the image you present.

In sports officiating, there are preferred ways of operating—ways that tend to lead to success, although there are no guarantees. The ways you choose to operate are revealed in the style you adopt. Three styles are described, but they are not mutually exclusive. You may find yourself justifiably adopting a particular style to fit the occasion. Because games vary widely in the skill level of the players and in intensity a good official readily adapts to the situation. This chapter also contains suggestions for beneficial personal behavior—ways of responding that are shaped by one's attitude, performance principles, and 10 commandments of style. Absorbing the ideas presented in this chapter should go a long way in helping you react to game situations in a positive fashion.

Three Styles of Officiating

It is important to recognize that the following definitions of officiating style are somewhat arbitrary, in that no one operates entirely in one mode all of the time. In fact, the key to successful officiating is flexibility in adapting your style to the specific situation. Officiating is very much governed by context, which means that a superior official adjusts his or her approach according to the type of game being played. Styles can change, even during a single game. With a knowledge of *how* to change, an official can make adaptations to fit the circumstances.

Rule-Book Style

Some officials say, "You can always hide behind the rule." If a potential violation by a player is borderline, it is always possible for an official to apply the most stringent interpretation of a rule and thereby have a bona fide excuse for ruling against the player.

Stringent interpretation of the rules, however, may not always be the fairest way to judge the action. Consider the slide in baseball or softball, for instance. The rules state that a runner must slide into home plate if a fielder is in position to make a play there. The runner is not permitted to come in standing up, because the catcher is in a stationary, vulnerable position and a collision may result. Therefore, the runner can be called out for failing to slide. Let's say that a runner is trying to score on a hit to the outfield, but the throw toward home plate forces the catcher to move up the third-base line. The ball and the runner arrive in the vicinity of the catcher—who is several feet up the line—at nearly the same time. To avoid the catcher, the runner deftly pirouettes around the fielder and steps on the plate without being tagged. The umpire could call the runner out for not sliding. However, if the runner

Sometimes you need to interrupt a contest for consultation. Wise officials, such as Don Wedge (left) and Dale Hamer, shown here, communicate to assure they agree on a call or a rule interpretation.

slides, causing the catcher to topple over and drop the ball, the runner could be called out for interference. In effect, the runner cannot win, even though, in fairness, the run should have counted. Any act at that point could have been called illegal, because of an off-kilter throw by a fielder.

We can imagine a dozen different scenarios about collisions or near collisions on plays at home plate. The rules cannot cover all these situations succinctly. They can only describe parameters. An official can take those parameters and apply them to the letter and, in effect, penalize players in a way that amounts to unfairness. Applied in an overly rigid manner, rules of play can actually be used to sabotage their intent.

Some officials operate that way. They think that by applying rules in a punitive manner, they are fulfilling their role as the game's guardians. But the rules of any sport are subject to wide interpretation simply because there are so many variations in game circumstances.

As an example of a rule that allows considerable latitude in interpretation, blocking in football used to be done with the shoulder pads. Players kept using their hands to push, however, and finally the rule makers made "pushing" legal. But the shoving had to be done "within the frame" of the body of the player being blocked. What is within the frame? An official who wants to apply the definition stringently can call "illegal use of hands" a lot, even if the contact has no bearing on the result of a play. In other words, a rule-book-style official could interrupt play almost at will, and some officials do just that, believing themselves to be conscientious. Players, coaches, and fans often find their overly strict judgment annoying.

Some rules, however, do not permit any deviance. The clearest examples are the rules regarding the boundary lines, which confine a sport and define its critical areas. When a ball possessed by a runner crosses the plane of the goal line in football, it is a touchdown, with no room for equivocation. When a batted ball hits a base in softball or baseball, it is a fair ball. When a basketball bounces on a sideline, it is out of bounds. Accurate perception—which is not always easy—is the determining factor in these judgments.

Although a strict official may be short on discrimination skills, some coaches like an official

Bending the Rules

Rules say that only captains may be present at the coin toss in football. But in one Vermont community, the "Pumpkin Queen," honorary Miss Cinderella, traditionally bursts from a papier-mâché replica of a pumpkin on the weekend of Halloween to conduct the coin toss. As it has been a tradition for many years with no detrimental effect on the game, officials invariably permit this ceremony. The rule was designed to curtail excesses, for example, having all the seniors march out to call the coin toss, which could be considered an effort to intimidate opponents.

who operates by the book, as long as he or she is even-handed and is equally picky with both teams. In games that flow rapidly, such as soccer, hockey, and basketball, an official who calls a tight game can hamper teams that play aggressive defense. Consequently, an official who administers hard justice will find a favorable reception in some quarters.

The Laissez-Faire Official

Some officials like to let players just play, without interfering very much. This is not an undesirable style as long as games move along smoothly. The difficulty comes when games become heated or when complicated judgments are necessary. The "live-and-let-live" official may get into trouble by not making calls when they are essential, not attending carefully to the welfare of players, or making a half-hearted decision when a crisp one is called for. Feeble decision making can be the undoing of an official.

The reasons officials operate this way are perhaps just as important as the results. One reason is that the official may not know very much about the game. The rundown in baseball or softball serves to illustrate this. If a runner is caught between bases, with fielders trying to make a tag, to free herself she may throw up her arms and try to hit the ball while it is being tossed between fielders. This is interference, and the runner should be called out. But a clever runner may know that if she can run into a fielder who does not have the ball, the fielder should be called for obstruction and the runner awarded safe passage to a base. An umpire who does not know these restrictions may offer no call at all, and hence the

Dick Creed at work. Smiling and talking lightly with players show that you're comfortable, confident, and at ease.

essence of the rule has been denied. Lack of rules knowledge, particularly those rules which seldom need to be applied, is a prominent shortcoming of many officials. It is one reason for what some would call lackadaisical officiating.

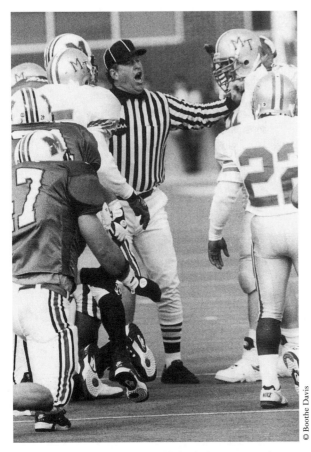

College football official Stephen McBride demonstrates how to use persuasion to keep problems from erupting on field. Sometimes authority must be vigorously asserted to maintain order.

Umpires in baseball and softball say that there are times when a vigorous "punch-out" is necessary to sell a call. Selling calls with vigor and dispatch is necessary at critical moments in all sports. An official whose timing is slow, whose signals are lethargic, and who fails to be emphatic at critical times is going to lose the confidence of players and fans. Coaches, too, despair over the official who just seems too nonchalant, inattentive, or deficient in courage to make sharp, strong decisions. The official who doesn't want to interfere—or is unsure of how to do so—can be a menace to the welfare of athletes.

Some officials go to games just to act as a decoration. They want to get the game over quickly so that they can collect their check and be on their way. They deliberately bypass calls because making tough calls would hold up the game. Unlike officials who are ignorant of the rules, these are often hard-bitten veterans who don't really care much about being conscientious. It is disheartening to report that some sports officials are less than dedicated, but in fact some officials let things slide because they just don't want to bother.

Laissez-faire officials are good only when the players themselves take control and run games satisfactorily.

Another shortcoming in officials is lack of hustle. Hustle means that an official can accurately process the goings-on in a game and anticipate where to be to make calls properly. Many officials don't know when to hustle and how to hustle. Hustling demands an intense dedication to being in the right position from which to view a play. Sometimes declining to hustle means that the official really can't hope to make a sound call.

Players should be warned if they make a hard tag in baseball or softball; if they commit a hard foul in basketball; if they come close to executing an illegal, punishing hold in wrestling; or if they are close to committing a dead-ball foul in football, such as jumping on top of the pile after a runner is downed. An official who refrains from warning players about potentially dangerous acts is either ignorant of the danger or reluctant to take action. Just wanting to let people play is a poor excuse for not being diligent.

Advantage/Disadvantage Officiating

Naturally, the best officials are those who have a deep sense of what the game is all about, are on top of the rules, and have a healthy respect for the players and the game that they are officiating. Their basic intent is to take charge of a game and run it as smartly and efficiently as possible, letting the players play when only minimal intrusion is necessary but intervening in a decisive way when events in the game show that measures of control need to be applied.

Even-handed could be one way to describe such officiating, but perhaps a better name for it would be *advantage/disadvantage application of the rules.* Officiating manuals invariably contain a section that advises officials to follow the spirit of the rules and not to act like overzealous enforcers of the letter of the law. One cannot keep a rule's spirit, though, without a keen knowledge of what that spirit is. The key to going with the flow of a

College football official Butch Lambert exhibits the kind of focus necessary in officiating.

game is a thorough grasp of the sport's ideals. What constitutes a good game? How can players be guided (rather than forced) into playing a fair, fervent contest? When does an act that borders on a violation stop short of giving one team a decided advantage? The following examples illustrate situations in which a good official must apply the advantage/disadvantage principle.

▋ In basketball, a player dribbling down the floor is met by a defender whose arms are outstretched. The dribbler executes a skillful crossover dribble and slides by the defender, although the defender's arm swipes across the body of the ball handler as she moves.

▋ In soccer, a defender slides feet first toward a player dribbling the ball and momentarily causes the dribbler to disengage. But the dribbler hops aside, even though the defender's slide caused a slight imbalance, and moves downfield in possession of the ball.

▋ In football, a wideout moves into the defensive backfield and cuts in front of a defender on what looks like a pass route. As the wideout

moves past the defender, the defender sticks out his arms and gives the potential pass receiver a small shove outside the frame of his body. The play is a "draw," however, and no pass is thrown.

In each of the preceding cases, a discriminating official would say that although contact was technically illegal, in the spirit of the game no advantage accrued. This is not to say that possibly harmful acts should be overlooked. The point is that a genuinely savvy official makes distinctions about play action and penalizes behavior that is clearly illegal while bypassing calls on action that doesn't impinge on the spirit of the rules.

It takes a very strong official to function this way and still retain staunch integrity. It means that an official must make discrete judgments about a game's intricacies. It means, too, that a considerable amount of experience is necessary before an official can reach this point of making rapid-fire, astute decisions. The judicious no-call is sometimes the best call of all. Officials who approach this point in their development are considered top of the line. The middle way is usually the superior choice.

Preventive Techniques

Preventive officiating takes two forms. One is helping players avoid technical violations. A basketball official, for instance, will withhold the ball from a player on a throw-in if that player's foot is on the boundary line. A baseball or softball umpire may notify a pitcher if that player is close to delivering an illegal pitch, say, with improper footwork on the rubber. A football wing official will often put one foot out in an effort to guide a split end, showing the limit of the so-called neutral zone.

The second preventive technique is a method of notifying a player not to commit a foul. Sometimes fouls are the result of inadvertent player behavior. Charging into the snapper on punts is one such action in football. Rules protect the snapper, who is in a vulnerable position after he's put the ball in play. Sometimes a fielder will absent-mindedly stand in a base runner's path in softball or baseball, and an umpire can advise against it. A basketball player can be told to avoid excessive hand-guarding or to avoid elbowing on rebounds. In this way, officials act to prevent player-to-player contact that could result in fouls.

Any warnings to players about potential violations should be issued during dead-ball intervals, although it is sometimes possible to call to players during live action, as when telling football players to stay off a runner whose progress has already been determined.

Context Determines Approach

Dr. K. Lee Kuhlke of Englewood, Colorado, is a specialist in prosthodontics, a dentist who straightens people's bites. As one of the top soccer referees in the state, he also specializes in taking the "bite" out of aggressive soccer players. But his point of view illustrates the firm control an official must occasionally exercise over sports competition. At times, an official has to take a stance about the way a game should be handled even before the game begins. Dr. Kuhlke explains that context is key:

> Depending on the level of play and the intentions of the players, we can assess the situation and either call a "loose" game or else revert to a "tight" style. A lot depends on degrees of player skill and the intensity of rivalries. I had an adult match of players who were of Turkish background against a team composed largely of Greek immigrants. It was fought on American soil, of course, but there was no affection between opponents.

Though no nationalistic loyalties or animosities are likely to surface in high school competition, schools often have rivalries, and sometimes those rivalries have an underlying basis in the background of the populations they serve. Competing schools may serve youngsters from families of different social or economic backgrounds, religions, races, or points of origin, all of which may play a role in how students view opponents.

Rivalry could—and often does—arise between schools that are near each other, a community envy of sorts. Proximity sometimes creates longstanding rivals, which brings up another point about context: Sometimes lingering anger is the result of an unpleasant incident between schools, which may have happened years ago or only a week before.

How can an official know of a history of animosity or rivalry? Often the official does not know, and in some ways that is good, because the official can approach the contest with pure neutrality. But if an official does know of a potentially hostile atmosphere, such knowledge can alert the official to be wary, to have his or her "antenna" tuned to possible expressions of ill will and acts of retaliation.

At the other end of the emotional scale, a game atmosphere of complete frivolity or a careless attitude on the part of competitors is sometimes dismaying for officials. Perhaps coaches and players alike aren't really taking the game seriously. Officials may feel left out because whatever they call won't matter much to the participants. But this situation is rare; most people who bother to practice and suit up generally take their roles very seriously.

Another kind of competition that challenges officials features players who are inept. Sometimes a school traditionally hasn't had much success in a given sport, the sport is new to the program, or perhaps there is very little training in the activity below the high school level. It may be only one of the teams that is fundamentally poor, making the game lopsided. At any rate, when play is sloppy, officials have to adjust their expectations and operate according to the skill level of players, which may mean overlooking technical violations and making allowances for the lack of ability.

The best kind of competition is an intense game where players respect one another and are determined to give 100 percent toward the goal of victory, with no quarter given, but with an honorable outlook acknowledging that sportsmanship is just as important as a favorable outcome. This happens a lot at high school events, though newspapers don't trumpet such contests unless a league title is in the balance. Officials can testify that often the most-heated battles, fiercely contested but cleanly played, are between schools that have poor records. They play that way as a matter of pride, not wanting to be thought of as sour losers and trying to make their followers pleased with their effort. These are exciting games to officiate.

Style and Mechanics

Signals are fundamental communication devices for all officials. Officials convince others of their accuracy in judgment by the way they execute signals. Signals are the most visible embodiment of an official's style. They are an area where uniqueness stands out.

Good officials rehearse these telling movements; they check themselves in a mirror while gesturing to be sure of the image they want to project. Use professional officials as models. Watch how a major league baseball umpire removes his mask, how he observes a pitcher warming up, the way he brushes the plate, and the propelling motion he uses to cover another crew

© Jeff Soucek / IHSA

A call is "sold" by smooth, rhythmic, synchronized movements and forceful body language.

member's base. Watch how an NBA referee tosses the ball to a free-throw shooter. Notice how NFL officials release their flags, kill the clock, or obtain an out-of-bounds spot. See how a polished volleyball official notifies a server to put the ball in play. Observe when a wrestling official flops to the mat to check a hold. Many high school officials also exhibit sound habits to copy.

The timing, emphasis, clarity, presentation, and smoothness of signaling should be mastered as the rule books and manuals illustrate them. Move away from clusters of players. Avoid being loose-jointed, flippant, stiffly mechanical, or exaggeratedly demonstrative. *Mechanical* is stiff and spasmodic, with muscles taut. *Demonstrative* is striking a showy pose when only a minimal signal is called for, for example, waving a foul ball in baseball and yelling "Foul!" when a ball is hit into the stands, or using body English and a massive torso twist to denote a simple side-out in volleyball. If a basketball player knocks a ball out of bounds, the official's signal should not reflect the crowd's reaction, regardless of the context. The signal should be clear and measured but not exuberant. By the same token, touchdown signals or a change-of-possession indicator after a fumble in football should not carry a message that the official is somehow happy for the scoring or recovering team. "I don't care if he leaps in the air on touchdowns," one coach remarked, "as long as he jumps just as high for us as he does for our opponents." Don't rise off the playing surface when signaling.

On the other hand, firmly planted feet and a solid horizontal swipe are essential when calling a runner safe on a close play in baseball or softball. A strong thrust is also necessary when declaring a charge in basketball. In sum, the official must learn distinctions about when and how to execute the semaphore systems required in game administration.

Personal Characteristics

Some personal characteristics are likely to be instrumental in helping you become a good official. These qualities are not necessarily inherent, but you can work to adopt them consciously:

- Integrity—This involves choices you make while working always to uphold the highest principles.

- Courage—Many situations in games will test your ability to be brave and to make decisions that you know in your heart are correct but that may not be popular.

- Self-confidence—You should start off each game by giving yourself a pep talk about showing everyone that you are completely in charge.

- Decisiveness—Some judgments have to be made quickly and emphatically. When you execute such judgments properly, you gain the confidence of those involved in the game.

- Consistency—Each situation differs, to be sure, but strength of purpose is shown in the evenness with which you make decisions.

© Referee

Not many officials are as tall and physically imposing as Steve Welmer, but all officials can earn respect by hustling, knowing the rules, and being decisive.

- Being even-tempered—This may be the hardest attribute to achieve, because though it's easy to remain calm when nothing is happening, it's hard to do so when people react negatively to your performance.

- Humility—There is a tendency among some officials to adopt an authoritative, defensive posture, but the official who gains the most respect admits that sometimes he or she could be wrong.

- Understanding human nature—Some people whine when they are aggrieved, and they're usually sorry for it later; try to forgive them before they ask for forgiveness.

- Ability to control situations—When something odd happens in a game, pause to replay the event mentally, then make a firm decision, and resolve to convince others, in a soft but direct way, of the sense behind your decision.

■ Hustle—There is no substitute for dashing to position yourself for a firm call, and people will appreciate that you're on top of the play, even if they don't say it.

Personal Performance Principles

In addition to the characteristics mentioned in the previous section, there are a number of additional pieces of advice to guide your behavior. These guidelines produced by *Referee* magazine will affect your officiating style positively.

■ *Be competitive.* The players give maximum effort; so should you—every game. Remind yourself to stay on top of play and to pay attention to peripheral happenings, such as harsh talk among participants, sniping from the sidelines, and overreacting by the crowd. You are hired to make calls that control the game.

■ *Have your own head on right.* Your uniform and position in the game do not grant you immunity from criticism. Effective officials know how much to take before responding, and knowing where to draw the line is essential. Be assured that a line of tolerance must be drawn at times in order to prevent intimidation.

■ *Avoid a showdown.* If a coach is relentless in negative remarks, stay as far away as possible. This is especially important during breaks in action. Don't invite a blowup. Moving near an irritated party just to show who's in charge will only lead to further acrimony. Some officials adopt a defiant attitude that erodes respect from participants.

■ *Get into the game's flow.* Make efforts to understand the game's tempo and to recognize the difference in speedups and slowdowns. At times, officials want to control the rhythm; at other times, they help accommodate or maintain a pace set by the teams. A ragged game demands a different style of officiating from a smooth one.

■ *Never bark.* This is a Golden Rule philosophy. No one likes to be yelled at; it sets the recipient on edge and increases tensions. Apply this philosophy when dealing with others. Be firm when necessary, but use a voice with a modulated pitch. Shouting appears to be defensive and indicates a loss of personal control.

■ *Show confidence.* Know the line between arrogance and confidence. Your presence should command respect from participants. A sharp appearance, a smooth manner, erect carriage, and a polished voice determine whether or not you'll be readily accepted. Image is indeed important, and body language speaks louder than words.

■ *Forget the fans.* The audiences at games tend to exhibit three pronounced characteristics: ignorance of rules, highly emotional partisanship, and delight in berating officials. Accepting that will help you to ignore the crowd and concentrate on the job at hand.

■ *Answer reasonable questions.* Courtesy is a vital technique for an official. Treat coaches and players with politeness. Use formal words, never curse, and make listening a strong element in any

Umpire Greg Schmidt watches a play unfold in a high school softball game. Good officials make sure they see the *entire* play before making the call.

personal exchange with game participants. Be firm, be gentle, and be relaxed. Weigh each word carefully when answering questions or reacting to challenges. It is impossible to take words back once they have been uttered.

■ *Stay cool.* One goal is to establish a calm environment for the game. Edgy officials are easily spotted by fans, coaches, and players. Animatedly chewing gum, fidgeting and pacing nervously, or being overfriendly will make you appear vulnerable to pressure. Indecisiveness can be your downfall. You will be judged the instant you step into the playing area. Therefore, don't greet acquaintances in the stands enthusiastically (your actions may easily be misinterpreted), and avoid throwing your head back in amusement. Your role is not that of an entertainer. Instead, adopt a formal, respectful, businesslike approach to everyone connected to the game. That way, respect is likely to be returned to you.

The Power of Body Image

You can't alter your genetic make-up, but you *can* control some things about the way you look. You can control your grooming, your manner of speaking, your gestures, and your body posture. You can also take charge of your personal eating habits and your use of tobacco. If your ordinary walk is a shuffle, you can strive to step in a more sprightly fashion. If you have a tendency to slouch, merely by being conscious of the problem you can work toward a cure by throwing your shoulders back. An upright posture—head erect, with toes pointed forward in a brisk and purposeful stride—is characteristic of top-notch officials. Fresh uniforms (not ragged or faded), polished shoes, carefully groomed hair, and a somewhat jaunty manner of moving are also emblematic of superior officials.

Certain less-than-conservative forms of dress and presentation are sweeping the country today. Young people have embraced the grunge look on a wide scale: baggy clothing, languid walk, body piercing, and tattoos. Major league baseball players seem to favor five o'clock shadows. Some NBA performers appear to be mobile signboards with their body etchings. But if an official shows up at a game with a nostril ring, people are likely to look at him with a sneer. If an official has a safetypin through her cheek, she is apt to draw cold stares and a few expressions of disbelief whenever she makes a close call. In short, some fashions that are acceptable in society at large are not likely to be considered proper for sports officials. Basically, officials are held to more conservative, clean-cut standards. Moreover, if you smoke or chew tobacco, do it somewhere other than near the playing facility.

A Confident Decision

In a state play-off game several years ago between East St. Louis and Alton, Illinois, football referee Len Scaduto dealt with a controversy in the following way. The game was stopped for an official team time-out, and a coach beckoned the referee to the sideline.

The coach said that a crisp pass to an end had been trapped on the last play, although no official had declared the pass incomplete. "I'll check it out," said Scaduto. The ref then gathered the crew in the middle of the field and asked what each member had observed, whereupon they verified that it was a good catch.

In reporting the decision to the coach, Scaduto added that he felt the officials had good angles and that he had complete confidence in their judgment. This judicious pause on the part of referee Scaduto indicated that he himself had enough self-confidence to pursue the matter seriously and that he was also convinced that he'd get straight answers from his crew. Scaduto's strong presence of mind was also shown in his willingness to listen to the coach's contrary perception and then securing a satisfactory resolution of the issue.

Hockey official Derek Martin signals that a player is not offside. The way an official uses accepted gestures to indicate judgments puts a special stamp of confidence on personal conduct.

The 10 Commandments of Style

Here is a list of style rules to keep in mind at every game:

1. Avoid criticizing other officials; even without your contribution, there will be a sufficient supply of criticism.

2. Avoid second-guessing game strategy; many others feel it is their own right.

3. Strive to avoid the appearance of favoritism; smile, but don't laugh out loud. There should be no such thing as a friendly, neighborhood official.

4. Most signals should be preceded by a distinct pause. Avoid overreacting; instead, make signals rhythmic and snappy.

5. Recognize when you've made a controversial call, and permit reasonable disputation. Realize that you are arbitrating a *competition.* Listen before you respond, but never tolerate a personal attack such as name calling.

6. When in doubt about a ruling, make a firm decision, explain your reasoning, determine the truth later by referring to the rule book, then reveal your findings accurately and promptly.

7. Never invent calls; be sure of what you observe. See the whole play.

8. Don't bluff; if you don't have an answer, admit it. To be *positive* is to be wrong at the top of your voice.

9. If a judgment call deserves an explanation, provide it.

10. Never be neglectful, cavalier, or nonchalant about your image; people are observing you, and they'll admire a professional demeanor.

Summary

Blending may be a key word for this entire chapter, because you will succeed as an official if you combine many facets in your approach to handling athletic contests. For one thing, you must learn to blend different styles according to the type of competition in which you are immersed. Sometimes you can be strict, sometimes you can be lenient, and often these shifts in approach take place within the same game without sacrificing consistency. Officiate the game the way the game is being played, which means using the advantage/disadvantage principle wisely.

You must also fortify your personality with characteristics that reflect your strength of purpose, which means blending attributes of self-confidence, tact, assertiveness, and understanding. These ways of dealing with others can be consciously chosen, particularly if you think before reacting. Your chief aim as a sports official is to become a sound decision maker in the midst of athletic competition, while maintaining poise and convincing participants of your integrity.

The next chapter introduces some of the goals for which you can reasonably strive. Learning to set and achieve realistic goals can help you plot the course toward improving as a sports official.

3

Goal Setting

George Selleck

In this chapter you'll learn

- seven common mistakes about goal setting,
- 12 factors to consider when developing goals, and
- seven sensible goals for sports officials.

"If you don't know where you're going, you may not get there," a wag once remarked. He might have added that with faulty planning, you're likely to end up somewhere else.

Planning the Future

In terms of looking to the future, how you conduct yourself will, to a great extent, be based on what you want to accomplish on a daily, weekly, annual, and career basis. Your officiating goals, which are personal and based on your own hopes and expectations, should be dynamic. That is, they should evolve—one goal leading to another

once it has been met—and they should change only after you carefully assess the need for change. If you should step from one level to another, say, from subvarsity to varsity games, once you arrive at the new status, you may ask, "Where do I want to go from here?"

Goals should be familiar to anyone who has participated in sports. Everything about sports is goal oriented. The most significant aspects of sports are setting, striving for, and achieving goals.

For example, successful coaches continually set goals and methodically go about trying to achieve them. A varsity basketball coach is likely to tell herself before the season begins that she wants her entire squad to

- be in good shape to carry out a full-court press for an entire game,
- make a least 75 percent of their free throws,
- learn two systems of half-court traps,
- rebound 25 percent of their own missed shots,
- master a semi-fast break off a rebound,
- master two attack plans for specific zone defenses,

Pick your spot—home plate ump in softball or wearing the white hat in a Super Bowl—set realistic goals, and then work to reach them.

- learn at least three alternate inbounds maneuvers against presses, and
- master two end-of-game offensive plays designed to produce a high percentage shot.

Naturally, this list could go on. The coach could list a win/loss goal, for example, or a more abstract goal, such as trying to develop players' ability to think for themselves on the court. Of course, not every coach goes so far as to draw up such precise goals as these. The ones who do, however, are generally known as winners.

Officials can also follow the same sort of detailed approach to preparing for their season. A wrestling official may say before the season, "I am going to read one coaching book so that I become familiar with how holds are taught. I'll have one strategy session with a coach and two with a fellow official to learn combat techniques and officiating tactics. Once a week for 10 minutes, I will practice my signals in front of a mirror."

Success—whether off or on the court—begins with clear goals. A study at Yale University in 1953 found that only 3 percent of that year's graduates had set specific career goals. Twenty years later, in 1973, that 3 percent proved wealthier and had accomplished more than the other 97 percent combined. Without clearly defined goals, many people merely drift through life, hoping they'll bump into success along the way. They embrace the philosophy of the poet Milton, who said, "They also serve who only stand and wait."

Are you one of those who play the "waiting game"? A good way to find out is to ask yourself questions such as these: Why did I go to school? What made me choose this particular career? What have I expected to accomplish in my career? Do I have a mental picture of where I'm going in my career? Does my job fit my personal aptitudes? How did I get my previous jobs? Did I actively pursue them, or did they more or less fall into my lap? What skills do I have and how did they come about? Your answers to these questions should give you a clue as to whether you are someone who waits for things to happen or someone who makes things happen.

Everyone realizes that goals are important, yet a surprising number of people have no clear personal or professional goals. Instead, they just drift along, hoping they'll somehow bump into suc-

No Empty Promises

In a recent commercial for a political campaign, an incumbent gazed steadily into the television camera and said, "I want to look every voter in the eye and say I've worked diligently for your welfare. I won't let you down!" You too can say, "I'll be the best official I can be," but the expression will be as empty as a politician's promise if you don't fill in the blanks by specifying carefully how you are going to reach a well-defined point.

You Get What You Reach For

People with just a vague notion of goals may reach a plateau and then remain there for lack of incentive to push forward. Or they may be content to rest at a certain level. Each person sets the mark for personal achievement. One person's goals may not fit another person.

A pair of basketball officials from Elgin, Illinois, were considered hotshots by the officiating fraternity because they had a strong way of controlling games, even though they were both under 25 years of age. They worked a state play-off championship tournament together before they were 30.

But just one of them had a burning desire to rise further. He approached other officials about working college football and was invited to help with spring scrimmages. Later, he got a small college schedule and then moved up to a major conference. His partner continued to work high school football and basketball games. The ambitious individual, Larry Nemmers, eventually became an NFL referee.

cess along the way. Goals crystallize thought and provoke action. They keep you focused on what is important and help you make good decisions. You are in better control of your life when you have goals toward which to work. Setting goals is the key to performing at your peak.

As you contemplate the prospect of officiating sports, you might first take an assessment of your personal attributes and then set some general standards for what you'd like to do. Ask yourself a few pertinent questions such as, Do I like a particular sport? Do I have a personality that will adapt readily to the difficulties of officiating a sport? Do I know enough right now to enter this avocation at a low rung? Am I willing to make a commitment to learn? Will I settle for mediocrity, or do I want to be a top-notch performer?

Common Obstacles

Just setting goals doesn't guarantee that you will achieve them. Saying to yourself, "I want to lose 20 pounds this year so that I'm not huffing and puffing up and down the court," and then going about life as usual will not make you 20 pounds lighter by the time the year-end tournament rolls around.

In his best-selling book, *Psycho-Cybernetics*, Dr. Maxwell Maltz compares the goal-setting process to the homing system in a torpedo. Once the torpedo's target is set, the self-adjusting system constantly monitors feedback signals from the

target area. Using the feedback data to adjust the course setting in its navigational computer, the torpedo makes the corrections necessary to stay on target. If programmed incompletely or nonspecifically or aimed at a target too far out of range, the torpedo erratically wanders around until its propulsion system fails or it self-destructs.

What kinds of things do people do that get them off-target when it come to achieving goals? These are some common mistakes:

▌ Not saying how you will measure your progress.

Example: "I'll read the rule book." Does this mean you'll read a chapter a day? A sentence a day? When do you plan on finishing the book? Before the season starts? Before the season ends? Before you retire?

▌ Setting a goal because someone else really wants you to.

Example: "This year I'll attend that officiating clinic my supervisor keeps bugging me about." How much do you think you will get out of the clinic with that attitude? It's possible to achieve goals that we set because other people want us to, but it's not much fun. The most meaningful and enjoyable goals that we achieve are the ones *we* want to reach.

▌ Setting goals that conflict with one another.

Examples: "I want to project a firm, authoritative manner," and "I want all the players and coaches to like me." When you set goals, examine them carefully to make sure they don't conflict with each other. We most often set conflicting goals when we set goals that are not in line with our personal values (more about that later). When your goals are in harmony with who you are as a person, they will probably be in harmony with each other as well.

▌ Setting too many goals.

Example: "My immediate goals for this month are to officiate two games, paint the house, give the car a tune-up, take the kids camping, and regrout the bathroom tile." I have a friend who actually sets goals like this and then gets upset with himself because he only accomplishes one or two things or else gets bits and pieces of his goals accomplished but never completes anything. When you set too many goals, it is difficult to focus on the ones that are most important.

▌ Not setting goals because you're afraid.

Example: "I really should learn to control my temper better when a coach challenges me, but that's just the way I am." It may be the way you *are*, but it doesn't have to be the way you *stay*. Saying "I can't change" is just another way of saying "I don't want to change" or, more likely, "I'm afraid to try." This fear stems from two sources. One is the fear of failure that we learn as children. We're afraid to try because we're afraid we'll fail. The other fear we sometimes have is fear of *success*. In this case, we're afraid to try because we might actually succeed—and with that success will come a change in our outlook. The thought of that change often makes people uncomfortable.

▌ Setting goals that you're not willing to work toward.

Example: "I'll get in shape for the season by running five miles every day." Now, this is an admirable goal if you enjoy running and have the time and self-discipline to follow through. But if the thought of doing that much running raises goose bumps on the back of your neck that are not shivers of anticipation, then having a goal for which you're not willing to do the work is just setting yourself up for discouragement.

▌ Setting unrealistic goals.

Example: "I will never make a bad call." There are a lot of sports fans out there who wish officials would set this goal! However, everyone knows that even the best officials occasionally make a bad call. A better strategy would be to set goals that improve your officiating skills so that you can reduce the number of bad calls you make.

Setting and Achieving Goals Effectively

A Chinese proverb states that a journey of a thousand miles starts with a single step. The hardest part of accomplishing any goal is getting started. Remember the law of inertia from physics class? A body at rest tends to stay at rest. Fortunately, the opposite is also true: A body in motion tends to stay in motion. That's why I always find it helpful to break any goal into small, manageable steps. For example, a friend of mine who does her own taxes never sits down and does them in one day. ("Too depressing," she says). Instead, she sets one afternoon aside for gathering all her receipts and such, another for organizing the information, a third for figuring her deductions, and so on.

Start with small steps. As you accomplish each one, you will build the momentum you need to keep going. The following sections contain other tips for making the goal-setting process work for you.

Know Yourself

You cannot achieve goals that are inconsistent with your self-image. If you picture yourself as always officiating at a minor level, it is likely that you will stay at that level until you change your self-image. Similarly, if your self-image is that you have the skills and talent to succeed at a higher level, you are more likely to take appropriate steps to achieve your goals.

If you have a goal that is inconsistent with your self-image, you have two options: You can change your goal, or you can change your self-image. The bottom line is that you need to see yourself as someone who can achieve your goals. Without that vision, you won't succeed.

Dan Chrisman keeps a close eye on physical play near the basket during a college game. Expect to officiate a number of seasons successfully at the high school level before having the opportunity to reach the college ranks.

It is important to ask yourself, "Why do I want to be a sports official?" Answers might include to make extra money, to contribute to a sport you like, to benefit your community, to gain recognition, to engage in a vigorous activity, or even to advance to a high performance level (for example, college officiating).

Determine Your Needs Versus Your Wants

Your needs are those things that you feel are necessary for your personal well-being. Most people have a need for shelter, food, and clothing. Some people need things such as love, beauty, or a satisfying career. When it comes to setting goals, you should consider your needs your highest priority, because having them taken care of allows you to feel secure.

Your wants are those things that you desire but that aren't absolutely necessary for your personal well-being. For example, you may *need* to improve your level of physical fitness but not *want* to join a gym.

Identifying your needs and wants also means clarifying your personal values. What do values have to do with goals? Simple—if your goals are not in line with your values, you will be less likely to achieve them. When you make decisions that are consistent with your values, you experience a sense of comfort that you made the right choice. When your decisions are not aligned with your values, you usually feel uncomfortable about them.

To illustrate this, let's say you have set a goal to officiate at twice as many games as you did the previous year. You believe that this increased experience will help you quickly move up the officiating ladder. At the same time, one of your important values is family togetherness. You discover that you are not comfortable with spending this extra time away from your family. Since your desire to be with your family outweighs your

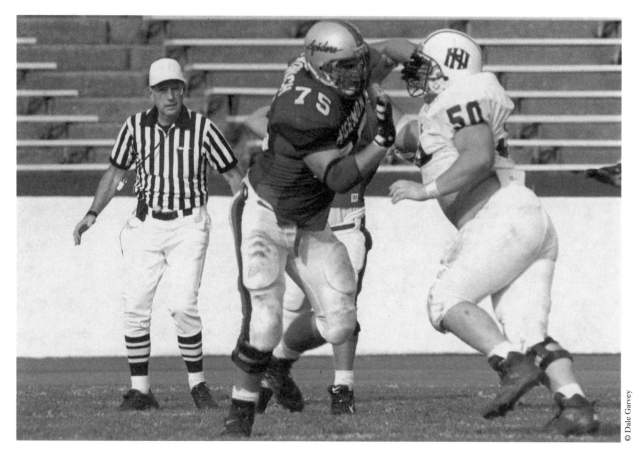

Referee Joel Goldman focuses on the blocking matchup between an offensive lineman and his opponent. It takes self-programming to train yourself to watch the "side plays" away from the main action.

desire to progress quickly in your career, you may need to reexamine your goals. You can generally tell whether your decisions are consistent with your values by how happy you are.

Establish Goals

You should have short-range, intermediate, and long-range goals. Short-range goals include daily and weekly goals. Intermediate goals include seasonal goals. Long-range goals include career goals, educational goals, and other life goals. As you achieve preliminary or short-range goals, you should reevaluate your intermediate and long-range goals. Sometimes these change as other goals are achieved.

Make Your Goals Specific

Be specific when you write down your goals. I like to say, "Be specific to be terrific!" Proper goal setting involves using the most specific parameters you can come up with; that way, your mind can work more efficiently for you. It's like using a computer. If you're too general when you type in the name of a computer file, you get the response, "No file found." You have to be clear enough about what you seek in order to find it. Here are some examples of vague goals versus specific goals:

Vague	*Specific*
I want to lose weight.	I want to lose 20 pounds.
I want to officiate more games.	I want to increase my number of games by 25 percent.
I want to learn the rules better.	I will memorize the first section of the rule book.

When it comes to improving your officiating performance, there are three areas to consider as you try to set specific goals. These are

1. your knowledge of the rules,
2. your adherence to accepted game techniques, and
3. your communication style.

A basketball official, for example, might decide that one specific way she can improve her knowledge of the rules is to put the dribbling rules into simplified but foolproof terms, so that it will always be possible to recognize a dribbling violation instantly. A baseball or softball official could say, "I want to be able to teach a newcomer all the complexities of base runner interference, in plain terms, along with enforcement steps." A soccer official might monitor his adherence to game techniques by saying, "During each long kick down the middle after an interception, I'm going to drift toward the sideline and try to get the proper angle on players converging as the ball comes down." An umpire who frequently finds himself in the middle of a tangled coverage situation ("What do you mean, 'Did I see that foul?' I thought you were on top of it!") could resolve to stop making assumptions about what fellow officials are doing and communicate every time it is necessary.

The important thing is to remember to spell your goals out clearly. If they are not set with precision, they are not likely to be reached.

State Your Goals in Positive Terms

You should always state your goals in terms of what you want to do, not what you don't want to do. For example, which statement sounds more encouraging to you?

■ I won't make a single bad call in this game!

■ I will follow player movements instead of looking to see where the ball is. That way, I will be more likely to make the correct call.

A goal should always be a positive thing to work toward, even if it's also challenging and difficult. In fact, goals usually are challenging and difficult, and that's why they need to be stated in positive terms.

Make Your Goals Obtainable

Sometimes people sabotage themselves by setting goals that they cannot achieve. Continuing failure to achieve a goal may be a signal that your goal is unrealistic.

You may need to review your tactics and time frames. It might be that you can achieve your goal if you give yourself more time or change the way you're trying to achieve it. Many officials have fallen by the wayside because they had unrealistic expectations of rising quickly through the ranks.

If you are a raw recruit, it certainly will be best for you to start officiating at the freshman or junior high level, depending on your locale. Sometimes subvarsity sports are operated in a casual, low-key, almost recreational manner, with few spectators and a philosophy that promotes playing large numbers of players. Some programs,

Officials who work games together can benefit by sharing and evaluating their goals. Your colleagues can help you set clear, measurable goals that you have a realistic chance of achieving.

though, feature highly competitive games where standings are kept and play is intense. You'll want to take a path that offers the smoothest route and the gentlest treatment of your own psyche. If you're not confident of your ability to cope with intense play, set your sights on a level that is challenging but does not exceed your abilities.

Sometimes circumstances surrounding you change more quickly than you or your environment are able to handle, and that affects your ability to achieve your goal. For example, a goal that previously had been obtainable might not be so after your wife unexpectedly has triplets. Or you might find that your local school district is eliminating several athletic programs because of budget cuts. Bad weather often causes cancellation of outdoor sports. A job change may squeeze the time that you have available to officiate, or an injury may curtail your schedule, meaning you'll have less experience at season's end than you had anticipated.

Make Your Goals Measurable

You make a goal measurable by setting objectives. An objective is a milestone in a plan for accomplishing a goal. It includes a time frame within which the objective is to be achieved and a method—a delineation of the steps necessary to achieve the objective. Having a goal without objectives is like planning to lose weight by saying, "I'll start losing weight on January 1, and by December 31, I will have lost 20 pounds." Each objective is a planned stop along the path toward your goal. In the example of losing 20 pounds, your objectives might look like this:

- I will exercise three times a week for 30 minutes each time.
- I will limit myself to one dessert per week.
- I will try to lose two pounds per month.

Some of your officiating objectives might look like this:

- By the end of two years, I will have worked at least a half-dozen varsity contests.
- In four years' time, I will be knowledgeable enough to help our beginners' coordinator train new officials.

- In seven years, I'll be working at the college junior varsity level.

Have a Feedback Mechanism in Place

Once you have goals and a genuine commitment to achieve these goals, the next thing you need is a way of getting feedback. Feedback is a basic element necessary for any type of goal achievement. How do you know when you're going in the right direction unless you get feedback?

Sometimes it will be obvious to you when you achieve a goal. For example, you step on the scale and it gives you the welcome feedback that you've lost another two pounds. Other times, it will be less clear. For example, if you set a goal to control your temper better, how do you know when you've achieved it? To determine whether or not you have reached a goal, you can ask an objective observer (a spouse, friend, coworker, etc.) to help assess your achievement.

Another way of obtaining feedback is to do a self-assessment periodically to make sure you are on the right track toward your goals. NFL officials are required to keep a game diary, which provides them with an effective tool for assessing their performance. You might want to consider doing the same. Another tactic would be to come up with a self-assessment questionnaire designed to address issues specifically that you feel are important to your personal and professional growth. Some questions you might want to ask yourself during this self-assessment include these:

- What levels have I worked at, and where can I go from here?
- Have I had enough game experience to move to a higher level?
- Do I listen and learn from criticism, no matter how it is delivered?
- Have I had to solve enough challenging problems during games to feel that I can rule correctly in difficult situations?
- Is my rules knowledge sufficient to carry me a step further?
- Are my game management techniques ingrained enough so that I can react without thinking?

- Are my game habits successful or counter-productive?

- Am I level-headed when stressful situations arise?

- Are my emotions under sufficient control that I can respond diplomatically when my judgment is questioned?

- Do fellow officials express confidence in the way I officiate?

- Have I had useful feedback from people who can judge my work thoroughly and fairly?

These are all questions you need to ask yourself as you determine whether your goals have been reached and what additional goals need to be set.

Know What You Need to Achieve Your Goal

Determine the resources you need to achieve your goal. Depending on your goals, you may need further education, increased officiating time, and so on. Resources can also be emotional. Desire is a resource. A supportive family is a great resource. Some resources are immediately available for use; others are not. What do you need? What do you have? How can you get what you don't have?

One exceptional resource for acquiring officiating know-how is to "tap the brain" of an experienced official. Many officials, especially young people, are reluctant to do that. Don't be afraid to ask a veteran official to offer some pointers. Suggest a lunch date and come prepared with a battery of questions. Many veterans find such an exchange satisfying, and you will find it enlightening. You'll learn about philosophy, how to deal with coaches, ways to advance, special game techniques, and methods of adapting to different partners. The price you pay for lunch might be well worth the "tuition."

Always Keep Your Goals in Sight

Florence Chadwick was the first woman to swim the English Channel. The first time she tried, she failed, even though she was just a few miles from the shore. Her problem? Heavy fog and choppy water prevented her from seeing the goal. The next time she tried, she kept a mental picture of the coastline in her head. This time, the fog did not deter her, because even when she couldn't physically see her goal, she could see it mentally. She kept her goal in "sight" until she finally achieved it.

Dee Kantner and Violet Palmer played basketball in college. Driven by their love of the sport and their competitive natures, they began officiating in games after they graduated. High school games were followed by college games, which were in turn followed by officiating in the WNBA. In 1997, Kantner and Palmer were welcomed into the officiating ranks of the NBA, becoming the first women to officiate in regular-season games in an all-male professional sport. Like Florence Chadwick, they kept their goal in sight, even when at times it must have seemed improbable that they would ever achieve it.

Be Flexible

Playing basketball taught me the importance of flexibility. Strategies should be used as long as they work. When the University of Utah played Arizona in the 1998 NCAA Final Four, Coach Rick Majerus knew the Ute's regular defensive strategy wouldn't work against the returning NCAA champs, so he went with a little-used triangle-and-two defense, which befuddled Arizona and led to a Utah victory.

If a particular strategy does not achieve your intended goal within a reasonable time, you should consider adopting another. When developing a strategy, it is important to be flexible. Circumstances sometimes change the usefulness of one strategy over another. When opportunities or obstacles (which may or may not have been anticipated) present themselves, you should be prepared to revise your strategy.

For example, let's say you're covering home plate, and a runner collides with you, breaking your leg. There goes your carefully planned schedule of officiating at a specific number of games for the season. But lost time doesn't have to be wasted time. Here is your opportunity to spend more time studying the rules or reviewing game tapes. Flexible people are those who focus on what they can do—not on what they can't.

Enjoy Meeting Your Goals

Do things that make the process of achieving your goals enjoyable. Do you remember those times as a kid when your coach said, "Hey, you guys have been practicing hard all week. Why don't we knock off an hour early today?" Didn't that feel great? Maybe you were lucky enough to have a coach who liked to interject a little fun into things—like a water-balloon fight at the end of a hot August workout. Experiences like these illustrate the importance of rewarding yourself for your effort. If studying the rule book is boring beyond all measure, promise yourself that after two hours of study, you'll let yourself read the latest Tom Clancy for an hour.

I always found that one of the bonuses of officiating was the opportunity to make new friends. A nice way to cement relationships between other officials and their spouses is to schedule social outings together—promise not to talk sports, at least not exclusively! Remember, pleasure is just as worthy a goal as improving your skill or elevating your status.

Don't make the mistake that many people do of thinking that you can reward yourself only after your goal is achieved. By taking time to pat yourself on the back as you work toward your goal, you make attaining your goal not only more enjoyable, but also more likely.

With life's rapid pace nowadays, stop to smell the roses. One way to savor an officiating outing is to take someone with you. If you have a long drive to the game, go early and take in a special sight or a snack. Stop afterward for a postgame review in a spot where you can bask in the glow of your splendid game. Make a cheery event of the experience.

Specific Goals for Officials

If you are a beginner in the field of officiating, you will probably find that your goals are relatively modest. These goals might include acquiring a basic knowledge of the rules and officiating procedure or obtaining a minimal number of game assignments. If you are an aspiring Little League umpire, for example, you might be satisfied with working a half-dozen games on the bases before trying to go behind the plate. You might also tell yourself that you'll learn all the rights and restrictions that apply to base runners. You might strive, moreover, to get 20 games' experience before the season ends. These are all realistic goals for a beginner.

After a season, you might wish to take stock of where you've been and where you are headed. Is it realistic to double your schedule of games next time around? Could you shoot for calling balls and strikes in half the contests? Is a postseason play-off assignment within reason? Would it be wise to ask for appointment to upper-level games, say, 10- and 11-year-olds rather than only 9 and under?

Here are some suggestions for other goals and objectives you might consider as an officiator; you will probably come up with more of your own.

■ I want to be better prepared for the game, including improving my physical conditioning, increasing my knowledge of the rules, and getting more officiating practice.

■ I want to improve my teamwork skills. I will spend time getting to know my fellow officials and observing their officiating styles.

■ I want to improve my communication skills. I will try to make three meaningful comments to players or coaches per game.

■ I want to improve my knowledge of the game from the perspective of others (administrators, coaches, and players). I will attend a minimum of two team practices to see how coaches teach and execute maneuvers.

■ I want to improve my self-control. When a coach voices a protest, I'll count silently to 5 before responding, and I'll keep the pitch and tone of my voice subdued.

■ I want to handle mistakes better. I will keep a game diary. If I make a mistake, I will try to determine what caused it (for example, not being in the right position or a lack of familiarity with the rules) and what knowledge I need to avoid making that mistake again.

■ I want to make the game a more uplifting experience for all those involved. I will not tolerate poor sportsmanship from the players, coaches, or spectators.

The Sweet Taste of Success

The harder you work toward a goal, the sweeter the taste of success. Remember that the road to success always has some pain or disappointment along the way. If you don't experience at least a little bit of stretching to achieve your goals, you probably haven't set them high enough to challenge you. And if your goals aren't high enough, then they may be holding you back.

When the road gets rocky, as it must, dig in your heels and focus on your goals. That is why it is important that your goals be *your* goals—not your spouse's, your parents', or your peers'. The people who persevere today are the ones who produce tomorrow. It is unusual in today's instant-gratification society to postpone what would satisfy us today for a promise of greater things to come. Don't sell yourself short by settling for less than your goals.

A natural goal for someone working in high school sports is to be assigned at the varsity level.

A next step is to acquire a substantial schedule, then an appointment to a big game, and eventually a play-off selection. Each of these steps is likely to be frightening. A philosopher once said, "If you're not scared by your next promotion, it probably isn't much of a promotion." Anxiety will increase as you move into places where a wider audience will notice your efforts. This "zing" should spur you to do a remarkable job. By showing an interest in officiating, you've already indicated that the limelight has an inviting glow. When a chance to advance arrives, force yourself through the qualms and embrace the challenge.

In Mitch Albom's book *Tuesdays With Morrie* (Doubleday, 1997, p. 56), a memoir of a former college student who attends his dying professor, Brandeis professor Morrie Schwartz says, "The biggest defect we human beings have is short-sightedness. We don't see what we could be. We should be looking at our potential, stretching ourselves into everything we can become."

Summary

Goal setting carries with it an obligation for developing a strategy to work toward what has been set and a willingness to strive positively to reach

Joe Baldino had to establish himself at a lower level before being assigned high school games. Reaching your full potential means being in the right place at the right time and taking advantage of opportunities as they arise.

that mark. Goals should be measurable. For example, not only can a goal of stating three complimentary things to participants during a game be measured, but its result can also be examined. Moreover, such positive goals are likely to have a salutary effect upon an official, providing a feeling of accomplishment. One positive goal can lead to several positive outcomes.

Honing your communication skills can be a worthwhile goal. The next chapter examines ways in which officials can improve their effectiveness in communicating.

Part II

Psychology of Officiating

4

Developing Your Communication Skills

Kay Roof-Steffen

There are three underlying truths about communication: It is inevitable, it is irreversible, and it is contextual. The manner, style, and content of all messages are a matter of conscious choice. The sender of messages can decide how messages are sent. The receiver may also, to an extent, make some choices about how messages are taken in.

When officials at the upper level of sports are observed in critical situations, they most often seem to be communicating in a calm, straightforward fashion. Effective communication techniques are learned; officials work very hard to respond sensibly to game conflicts and verbal attacks. They learn to weigh their words carefully, to develop mechanisms (expressions, gestures, posture) that convey a confident and soothing message, and to couch remarks in terms that solve problems rather than escalate them. Effective communication skills are vital to successful officiating.

Listening

There are essentially five reasons why people listen: to gain information, to empathize, to anticipate responding, to make judgments, and to enjoy the reception (entertainment). These are also the reasons that sports officials need good listening skills.

Much of what an official learns about a sport is gained through paying attention to what others

Listening may take the form of abject resignation, but at least the official, Dick Paparo, is standing by to take the heat.

officials. Information that comes to you verbally about how to work a game is likely to include suggestions for conducting pregame rituals, such as talking to captains.

In addition to learning about ways to start a game, listening carefully to advice from veteran officials will help you acquire special knowledge about anticipating unusual game situations, dealing with controversy, and working with game attendants, such as ball persons, scorers, and timers. Listening to learn is one of the most important functions of absorbing data.

Listening to empathize is another important purpose for paying attention. The idea of putting yourself in someone else's shoes means being aware of another person's emotions and understanding what their expressions signify—words as well as facial contortions, grimaces, smiles, frowns, and gestures of dismay, puzzlement, anger, and resignation. Listening carefully in many instances means more than processing sounds. It means listening with the eyes and heart as well. An official may try to remain neutral, but that doesn't forbid one from being receptive to the anxieties and frustrations of others. Good listening skills will help you understand *why* you are being challenged, helping you to empathize with those who do the challenging. Officials often say they must tune their antennae in order to pick up all the nuances of discord.

Once a coach or player explains an objection completely, the listening official must weigh the information, keeping a firm grasp of the other person's reason for making the objection. Often the reason may appear obvious: The complainant wishes the call to be reversed. But behind some objections are other factors, such as a coach trying to protect a player, trying to save face after a stra-

impart. In learning about the sport itself, you will want to take in the customary procedures for the way games are conducted. Rule books may specify formal practices, but actual operating conditions in your area will be passed on by word of mouth. Many on-field or on-court tactics for handling games will be told to you in person by other

Staying in Control

When most people are attacked verbally, their natural response is to defend and explain to counter whatever argument is offered. College baseball umpire Randy Christal of Austin, Texas, has adopted a technique that helps him to process what he hears. When a coach comes out to berate him for a call, Christal's response is, "What did you see?" That immediately switches the official's attitude to an empathic mode. Such a tactic will not come about if one relies solely on an automatic reaction. A person has to do some serious self-programming, however, to arrive at this controlled state.

tegic move goes wrong, or even seeking to obtain an edge on future calls through intimidation. Just as officials should "see the whole play," another piece of advice could be, "hear the whole story."

An official can separate the possible motivations of a verbal challenge by taking in the entire context of the message, analyzing the hidden messages, and trusting his or her instincts, as vague as these may be. The official's response usually takes one of two forms: to deny the challenge, which takes special skills in verbal diplomacy, or to offer a solution to the perceived problem. A solution may include consulting with an officiating partner or explaining a rule in clear and pointed terms. The key is to hear the problem in its entirety. Trying to solve problems by slipping into the viewpoint of an antagonist is a very hard part of officiating, and it doesn't come easily.

Many officiating judgments are based on what one sees, naturally, but sometimes they are based on what one hears. Let's consider a difficulty in a game already underway. A coach calls out, "That pitcher is throwing at my batters!" The context of the listening experience is perhaps the most vital element. All the following questions need to be considered: What time of the game is it? What is the score? What are the previous game circumstances that affect the present moment? How have you reacted to previous events? These central questions should pass through your mind while taking in the message and before arriving at a judgment.

Sometimes taking a deep breath before offering a response can help your mind process the entire context and permit you to arrive at a sensible determination. An enemy of effective listening is impulse, because impulse is often triggered by anger. Pause before talking and try adhering to the adage, "Engage brain before opening mouth." To monitor your own listening tendencies, keep track one day of how often you interrupt the talk of others. If you do it a lot, it means that you are in the habit of not waiting for the whole story.

Listening for pleasure is another dimension of the aural sense. It may seem odd that officials would listen for pleasure. Although you are not likely to take in the chirping of birds or a melodious symphony while working a game, some of the things you hear can be entertaining. Listen to what players say while in action; sometimes their remarks in the heat of battle are very funny. Many an official has also been moved by stirring renditions from the school band.

You can console players on occasion with a kind word or a pat on the arm. You can smile in amusement if their antics are humorous, without upsetting the continuity of the game. You can also

College ref Dick Burleson (now retired) listens to the complaint of former Arkansas football coach Danny Ford. Always try to lend an ear as long as the "discussion" doesn't delay the game. The coach may have a valid point that needs addressing.

empathize with their celebrations as much as you do with their disappointments. Officiating need not be an entirely impersonal role. People play games for fun or satisfaction; officials should have expectations of the same payoff.

Improving Your Listening Skills

The most important thing you can do is to adopt the practice of active listening. Emulate the childhood advice about crossing streets: Stop, look, and listen. Give a responder your full attention by planting your feet, keeping your hands still (a useful practice is to clasp your hands behind the back), leaning a little toward the speaker, and looking the speaker square in the eye. This attitude prepares you for message reception, but even this demeanor will not ensure complete receptivity unless you free your brain from its tendency to prepare a response before the message has been recorded.

Everybody prepares anticipatory scenarios in their heads. Usually those become stronger and more carefully rehearsed when people contemplate dealing with a crisis or an emotionally charged situation (such as asking for a raise in salary). What this means when someone is trying to "reach" you verbally is that you're more concerned with yourself and your reply than you are with the speaker's message. You have to plant yourself mentally in the speaker's position, push

aside your own latent reply, and turn yourself over to the person who is speaking.

Tuning out is another barrier to effective listening. When a coach or player approaches you with an issue, you may be mulling over something that just happened instead of focusing on the new message. Blocking previous events out of your mind so that you can avoid distractions and attend to the new problem takes practice. Tuning in means adopting the active listening mode previously described. It also means not guessing about the thrust of the new topic and not anticipating scenarios in your mind. Just open your mind to a fresh perspective and push mental clutter aside.

The process of "cleaning the slate" and opening the mind to new data is not an easy one. The first step is recognizing consciously a need to act deliberately rather than impulsively. The next step is to monitor your own thinking and reacting when you feel distracted: "Here is what I want to do. This is what I am doing now."

Letting emotions interfere with steady listening is another barrier to success. An angry word hurled by an athlete at an opponent or an official can trigger a negative emotional reaction by the official. It is almost impossible to listen dispassionately when you're mad, but how can you avoid it? Be conscious that your emotions are ignited. Talking to yourself can help you recognize your emotional state: "I'm getting angry. I refuse

Three Laws of Communication

Keep in mind these laws as you develop your communication skills.

1. *Communication is inevitable.* People react to your behavior, not what you intended to say.
2. *Communication is irreversible.* Once communication has taken place, it is impossible to undo it.
3. *Communication is contextual.* It takes place in six realms:
   a. Physical—in a specific locale
   b. Temporal—at a specific time
   c. Situational—under a given set of circumstances
   d. Psychological—with particular frames of mind, including historical factors (i.e., memory)
   e. Relational—how the parties are connected
   f. Cultural—why the parties are present (e.g., an exhibition game, a regular game, or a play-off game)

to let my anger escalate. I'll suppress my anger and shift into my active listening mode."

External noise is another barrier to effective listening. The key techniques in overcoming this barrier are to *filter* and *discriminate*. You must learn to filter out extraneous noise (the crowd, cheerleaders, loudspeakers, band) and attend to the messages you find important. Shut off all assaults of sound and just concentrate on working the game.

Verbal Skills

Verbal skills are essential in everyday life for securing one's preferences, negotiating personal alliances, building and maintaining relationships, and advancing a career. An official's status and progress are often determined by his or her degree of skill in spoken language. The question of how officials should talk comes down to an examination of the purpose of communication, with the psychological and cultural context in mind.

One purpose of pregame introductions with coaches and other game attendants is merely to get acquainted. Introductions often involve small talk about game conditions, the crowd, or the weather. The official should follow regulations by inquiring about conditions of the game site, the captains' names and numbers, special events connected with the game, and so forth. This is not the time to mention anything personal, and the official should avoid intruding on the private thoughts of coaches and game administrators. In preliminary procedures, officials should be direct, formal, and solicitous. They need information, and they need to set the stage for the game.

Once the game starts, any communication between officials and contestants or coaches—directives to players, answers to questions, warnings, responses to objections, and reactions to game situations—should adhere to the accepted practices for such interchanges. In all communications, including pregame discussions, words must be chosen carefully, lest the official's purpose be misconstrued. Diplomacy should be the guiding principle for officials' statements.

Officials must be aware of the denotation and connotation of words. An announcer at a game, pleading for good sportsmanship at the introduc-

© Travis Doster

Look like fun? Umpire Rick Neal may well have to eject coach Jim Thomas, but first he'll try phrases like, "I understand you're upset, but . . ." and "Coach, tell me what you saw."

tion of players, may refer to the visiting team as *guests*, implying that the home team as hosts should extend courtesy. *Visitors* is another soft or welcoming term. *Opponents* is a harsher name, although an accurate description of the visiting players. *Enemies* and *rivals* are more severe and judgmental designations. All these names for visiting contestants have denotations, which are the literal definitions, and connotative meanings, which add emotional dimensions to words and color the message conveyed because of people's feelings about the words.

If a coach complains while a game is in progress, an official might say, "I heard you, and I'll keep an eye out," to indicate that the coach may have a valid point. The official could also say, "I don't see it," "It's not there," or "I don't think so," to indicate that the protesting coach's message has been received but rejected. Compare the tone of these possible responses: "Oh, come off it!" "That's ridiculous," or "Whaddaya looking at?" These supercilious put-downs are improper for an official to use because they are attempts to cancel the protester's validity. But aren't those three expressions just the kinds of things a coach may say to an official? Yes, but it is the official's obligation *not* to traffic in kind. Sometimes an official cannot talk as other people do, because doing so would trigger further conflict.

An official should therefore consider certain expressions taboo. Among these are slang references to bodily functions or sexual behavior, cursing of even the mildest kind, name calling, negative adjectives ("worthless," "gutless"), and religious or racial slurs. Officials must choose their language carefully and, even in the heat of the game, adopt as neutral or formal a response as possible. It is also best to give strong negative messages with positive nonverbal reinforcement, such as a smile.

"I've heard enough" or "You've said enough" are about the strongest expressions an official should use to stop vocal harassment. It would be politic to preface such orders with "please." You cannot get away with saying "Hush your mouth" or "Shut up!"

Improving Your Verbal Skills

Here are three ways to improve your verbal skills:

1. Address people in respectful terms, even if you are responding to a disrespectful comment.

"Hey, buddy, stop calling me 'son'!" Many officials are oblivious to the importance of word choice. "Son" is patronizing and its connotation is negative, especially to a teenager. Perceptive officials avoid addressing players in demeaning terms, no matter the age of participants.

Choosing Words Carefully

An official defused a potentially explosive situation a few years back in a Clearwater, Florida, football game. Near the end of the game and with the score close, a quarterback faked a handoff and kept the ball himself, dashing around the end and down the sidelines. One official, however, thought that the player plunging into the line had the ball and blew his whistle sharply. He had ignored a fundamental axiom of football officials to "see leather," that is, to make sure that the runner had the football.

This mistaken whistle infuriated the coach, because it denied his team the tying score. Referee Ben Shlemon went over to the sideline and said, "I'm going to let you vent for a moment, and then we'll continue the game." The coach continued to scream awhile before his assistants tugged him aside. Shlemon then moved away so as to be out of earshot.

"Vent" is a term used nowadays to connote acceptable protests and rebukes, as opposed to such terms as *go crazy, go berserk,* or *have a fit.* The referee recognized that the coach was bound to be aggrieved, that the situation could not be rectified, and that a call of unsportsmanlike behavior would simply have compounded the problem. Shlemon also exhibited a firm resolve of closure when he indicated that game action would recommence shortly.

If a coach or player bellows, "Hey, that was a lousy call!" a soft reply ("The pitch was on the outside corner" or "She didn't establish position with both feet on the floor") is more convincing than a tart rejoinder.

2. Make explanations brief and to the point.

3. Avoid using technical jargon unless the terms are readily understood, such as "outside corner," "establish position," and "takedown."

Nonverbal Skills

Communication is not confined to language production. Just as spoken words should be chosen carefully, so too should body language be used in ways that promote positive outcomes. Body language—including gestures, facial expressions, body positioning, eye contact, and other visual cues—can actually overwhelm verbal messages. Officials who are fully aware of how their bodies transmit messages will take care to ensure that their nonverbal discourse is purposeful and clear.

Psychologists have tried to calculate the extent to which "actions speak louder than words." They have concluded that actions do indeed create a greater impact, 55 percent as compared with 45 percent for spoken language. When tone of voice, pitch, and tempo are added in the mix, the actual words used may have less than a 10 percent influence in communication. *How* something is said is therefore more important than *what* is said.

The phrase "Yeah, right" can illustrate the importance of nonverbal communication. The same words can express agreement or sarcastic and forceful disbelief. Facial expression, cast of the eyes, tilt of the head, curl of the lip, relative pitch and emphasis on each syllable, vocal tone, and time between words all operate to convey meaning.

Here is a simple exercise to demonstrate how different deliveries of a single sentence can convey a wide range of impressions. Read the following sentence aloud six times, the last time as a question, emphasizing a different word each time: *I did not do that.* Consider the meaning that is conveyed with each change of delivery.

A sports official should deliver as neutral and nonadversarial an impression as possible. The official should be perceived as one who is present to make things smooth. When challenged, officials should guard against using tone or gestures that appear patronizing. An officious or superior tone combined with haughty or disdainful body language, such as head tossing, eye rolling, jaw clenching, grimacing, and stiff limb movements, are sure to convey a negative message. Officials may think that their messages are not tinged with emotion, but without carefully controlling their movements and tone of voice, they are likely to reveal as much emotion as the player or coach on the attack.

Players and coaches recognize the quiet self-assurance of college official Ed Hightower through his words, actions, gestures, and facial expressions. These behaviors add up to a strong and effective officiating "presence."

Body Language Drill

Here is an exercise in using body language: Stand facing another person (or a mirror), and try to convey the following messages without words, using only your hands (held about chest high) and facial expressions. Notice that it will not take much imagination to create gestures; they come quite naturally.

1. A warning that a quarrel should cease.

2. A reply to an inquiry, such as a request for an explanation or more information.

3. A disclaimer, such as "I am unable to address that issue," or "That is impossible to rectify."

4. A denial of validity, such as "Your point is wrong."

5. A cessation or closure of communication, such as "This conversation is over; your plea is denied."

Awareness of discrete factors of nonverbal communication, such as simple hand gestures, can be of immense benefit for sports officials.

An official's body language has to convey his or her confidence in decision making when explaining a judgment call. An official must be aware of spatial elements, vocabulary choice, tone of voice, and body signals. Officials must strive for self-awareness to make sure all visual and auditory cues underscore their basic intent, which is to sell a call.

Improving Your Nonverbal Skills

Monitoring your own behavior is one way to improve nonverbal skills. Role-play the following scenarios with another person. Ask a third party to observe the exchange and assess the nature of the messages you delivered.

- A game administrator tells you there will be a special ceremony honoring parents before the game and asks for your cooperation. After the exchange, take a mental inventory of how you reacted. Did your movements signal a cooperative attitude or impatience?

- During a game, a player tells you that an opponent has committed an unfair act. Try to recall your facial expressions and upper-body motions while hearing the complaint and while responding. Recall and evaluate the phrases you used in responding.

- During a dead-ball interval, a coach says that you have missed a major violation. Analyze both your vocal and physical behaviors during this exchange.

Summary

There are two basic themes in this chapter. One is that officials must take pains to be receptive to messages aimed at them. Receptivity can be improved by practicing active listening and being aware of and overcoming barriers to listening. The second theme is that the way in which officials deliver messages is extremely important to their success. Officials should be aware of their spoken language and body language and try to use them effectively to convey their intended messages.

Along with sophisticated communication skills, an official needs sound decision-making skills in handling a game. The next chapter examines this topic.

An Official With Eloquent Gestures

A basketball coach in Manchester, New Hampshire, called from his spot on the bench to referee Joe Rolka, "My center is being obstructed. That guy sticks his knee out every time my player tries to pivot."

Rolka heard this complaint as he ran by. Without turning, he held out an arm, bent at the elbow, hand open, fingers spread and pointed upward, by which Rolka meant that he'd heard the objection and was taking it seriously but couldn't do anything at the moment. Rolka then moved down beyond the free-throw line, extended and dropped one shoulder, and then leaned forward from the waist to show that he was intent on observing the behavior he'd just been told about.

A moment later, still peering at the players on the court, Rolka again raised an arm toward the complaining coach and raised his index finger, indicating that he saw what the coach was complaining about but that it wasn't illegal contact at the present time.

At the next dead-ball opportunity, Rolka half-turned toward the bench, not making direct eye contact with the coach, but nodding slightly as he moved toward the defender. "Watch your knee. Let that man pivot once he gets the ball in there," Rolka said quietly as he moved past the accused individual, without looking directly at him.

This mini-drama by Mr. Rolka is enacted many times in a basketball season by polished officials. It features the official's acknowledgment of a complaint, a serious inquiry into the complaint's validity, and a remedial act that is both positive and unobtrusive. Rolka informed the coach through gestures that he was taking action and used body language to deliver his message discreetly.

5

Developing Decision-Making Skills

Jerry Grunska

In this chapter you'll learn

- the eight essential elements that go into making appropriate decisions and
- how to apply decision-making skills in game situations.

This chapter explores decision-making skills that officials need to become accomplished practitioners. It also presents ways to evaluate those skills along with suggestions for improving them. The emphasis will be on mastering the protocols and nuances of sport in an effort to administer games intelligently. You must absorb a considerable amount of knowledge and then be so steeped in the game's intricacies that the knowledge becomes ingrained and translates into rapid-fire, automatic decision making. When you make a call, you shouldn't have to think consciously about it.

Important decisions must be made throughout every contest, with perhaps the most vital ones being choices to do nothing, that is, allowing events to happen without interfering. Officials must learn to move with the game, and that includes anticipating plays so as to be in proper position to make calls. Officials must know which acts are legitimate and which are not. To be perceived as competent, an official must understand and promote the game's signature rhythms, must communicate decisions effectively, and must be able to work with partners. Games are often officiated by groups of officials. Officials must present themselves as a third well-synchronized team.

Here are the keys for making decisions during games:

- Know the rules.

- Know the language of the sport.

Francisco Plascencia at work at a high school soccer match. When possible, read the the strategy and tactics of the players, anticipating what events are about to take place.

▐ Master the signals, and employ them properly.

▐ Understand the game's rhythms and strategies.

▐ Be in proper position.

▐ Concentrate and focus on the essential elements.

▐ Remain calm.

▐ Work closely with fellow officials.

Know the Rules

Many experienced officials prepare for their season by reading the entire rule book each year. They refer to it throughout the season as well. The book is best studied in piecemeal fashion, one rule at a time or a few pages at a sitting. It really cannot be read like an adventure story; in fact, sometimes it is best to jump into the text at random instead of taking the sequential approach. For a beginner, trying to absorb its intricacies—even learning the rules language—can indeed be a challenge.

Perhaps the best way for a beginner to learn the rules and their implications is to attend a class

where the sport's jargon is introduced and discussed. Going over rules with an acquaintance is also useful, but the best system is to have a knowledgeable individual, such as an experienced official, explain the facets of seemingly simple definitions. Local associations also have rules study groups (officials may have to pass a yearly exam to remain certified in some states), plus they offer hints about on-field and on-court techniques, which are called *mechanics* (see chapter 12 for more information about associations for sports officials).

You have to be sure exactly what is permitted by the rules. Softball or baseball coaches may want to talk to pitchers, for example, and football and basketball coaches frequently call players to the sidelines for instructions. You must know when and how such communication is permissible. After a side-out in volleyball, you must know how much time a server may take before delivering the ball. After a foul strike in baseball, the limitations of a pitcher's motions before offering the next pitch are specified by the rules. When two wrestlers slide off the mat, you must have a clear notion of when to blow the whistle to hold up action and how to position the combatants correctly for renewing action. The average fan is unlikely to know all these requirements.

The average official, though, had better have them mastered.

Here are hints for learning the rules in logical order:

1. *Terms and definitions.* An official must know exactly what constitutes a legal screen in basketball, a legal pitch in softball or baseball, and a legal block in football. The definitions of these actions delineate what is correct and incorrect for proper rulings. Because the actions of players are swift, an official must have parameters firmly in mind when viewing such behavior. Definitions are at the heart of the game and must be memorized.

2. *Player rights and restrictions.* Descriptions of appropriate player behavior are extensions of the game's basic definitions. Football players may sometimes run with the ball after picking it up from the ground, but at other times they may not. A basketball player may retain possession of the ball after falling down in some very specific and carefully described circumstances. A baseball or softball player may run out of a baseline when certain conditions exist. An official must know what a player is free to do in order to execute accurate rulings.

3. *Violations and penalties.* When a player does something that the rules forbid, including acting in an unsportsmanlike way, consequences are spelled out in the rules. In soccer, when a kicked ball hits a player's hand, the rules describe how the circumstances govern the ruling. When a volleyball batted across the net strikes an opponent's head, the official must know instantly how to react. In football, a foul during a running play is penalized differently from a foul during a passing play, and spiking the ball is forbidden. The rules explain these differentiations, and they must be committed to memory.

4. *Description of the game, including scoring.* The rudiments of play may be well known by a person who has played the sport, but some intricacies of scoring may not be so clear. The football official must know how to treat a kick from placement that hits a goalpost. A baseball or softball umpire must know when to award a runner an extra base, just as a basketball official must know what constitutes a successful free throw. Descrip-

tions of playing and scoring cover the obvious purposes of teams, and they also explain the rare events that may not be clear at first glance.

5. *Dimensions.* Officials are not ordinarily expected to know playing surfaces' measurements or equipment specifications in detail. But they must be able to use the rule book as a reference in case irregularities are brought to their attention.

6. *Peripheral regulations.* In some sports, players' names and uniform numbers have to be recorded correctly in score books. Officials are responsible for approving this. In some sports, playing equipment is very precisely specified, as are requirements for uniforms and protective gear. Players are often forbidden from wearing certain items, such as jewelry or derogatory messages on their clothing. Officials have to learn what to permit and what to forbid.

7. *Rare occurrences.* An unusual event occasionally takes place during a game: several violations happen almost simultaneously, a ball lodges in an unexpected place, or a player does something peculiar, such as a football player coming off the sidelines to tackle a runner. The rules generally account for odd circumstances, and officials must know how to make decisions when a rare event takes place.

Know the Language of the Sport

Basic to any sport is its formal language, and the essence of this lies in the rule book's definitions of terms. A *bunt*, an *infield fly*, and the *strike zone*, for example, are very carefully defined in baseball and softball rule-book terminology. If you can recite the definition of the strike zone in rule-book terms, you have a better chance of getting it right consistently, just as recalling the definition of *traveling* may serve a basketball official. A wrestling official has to have the meanings of *takedown* and *escape* firmly in mind to make effective rulings.

Players' positions in the game have names: forwards, guards, tackles, fullbacks, quarterbacks, snappers, shortstops. Their play actions have names too: screening, dribbling, passing, batting, fielding, pitching, relaying, shooting, blocking, guarding. Officials have to know exactly what these designations mean in the rules in order to pass judgment on game maneuvers.

You must learn the rules lingo and be master of it; you must be able to speak this language and think in it, too. Rote memorization is the only route to a solid grasp of these fundamentals; a diligent reading of the sport's case book will then illustrate the application of these terms, that is, how the definitions operate in various game situations.

Master the Mechanics of Communicating Decisions

A basketball official blows a whistle to announce a foul. Immediately after sounding the whistle, the official has several prescribed steps to follow. Step one is pointing toward the feet of the accused player while raising the other arm overhead, hand clenched in a fist. Step two is remaining poised momentarily to observe any follow-through or retaliatory actions by players. Step three is turning to the scoring table and reporting the foul, a customary system of flashing the number of the offending player, the type of foul, and the ultimate result, either a throw-in from out of bounds or a free throw.

Each sport has such designated systems for announcing decisions. Sometimes they are solely visual, using arm and hand semaphores, and sometimes they include vocalization. In baseball and softball, for instance, it is important for an umpire to accompany a call at a base with a vocal notification, because the result of a call often furnishes the impetus for subsequent plays at other bases. In football, signals about the nature of fouls can be given silently—they speak for themselves—but many officials accompany their signaling with a verbal explanation to ensure that violations are communicated to the bench area. Verbalizing is also a good way for officials to assure themselves that they are administering the penalty correctly.

To demonstrate confidence in your decision, take the time to master hand signals and communicate them with authority.

Sometimes an official's decision in a game is a no-call. What may look like a foul from an onlooker's viewpoint may actually be a sportsmanlike act by a player: In football, an opponent may hold a punter upright so that he doesn't tip over, or a tackler may vault over a pile of players to avoid illegal contact. There are no designated signals for no-calls, but some officials use an open-hand gesture to notify spectators and coaches that they witnessed the act and have concluded that it was legal.

Though we can offer some advice, learning how to make game decisions is something you need to explore on your own in your specific sport. Keep in mind the advice in chapter 2 about learning what to call and what not to call.

You must also learn the sport-specific protocols for how and when to talk to players and coaches. You must learn when to explain decisions and when to let decisions speak for themselves. You must also learn when to ask for help from other officials during a game and when to offer help yourself, as discussed later in this chapter.

Adapt to Game Rhythms and Strategies

If a neophyte official has played the sport or followed it as a fan, he or she may already have a reasonable grasp of the game's rules and objectives. However, games have rhythms, rituals, and subtleties that a former participant may have forgotten or may never have learned. An aspiring official should become familiar with these ingredients of the sport to be in tune with its sophisticated aspects.

Proper tossing of the ball to start the game is a rare skill. Imaging helps you acquire the correct technique, but you'll also need to practice.

A football official should develop a regular pace in declaring the ball ready for play; a baseball umpire needs to speed things up by urging players to hurry to their positions between innings; a basketball official should put the ball in a player's hands rapidly for a throw-in. Tempo is a factor of many games, often determined by the players themselves but to some degree controlled by the officials. Officials should be aware of the game's inherent rhythms and try not to alter them. They should not intrude on the game unnecessarily.

Careless breaches of the game's tempo may annoy participants, coaches, and spectators. Their impatience may result in complaints, moans of anguish over routine calls, and even outcries of disagreement. Even many experienced officials are unaware of game rhythms; as a result, they may be puzzled at the expressed frustration from participants and spectators.

Some games are very intricate, and the official must be aware of the complexities to anticipate strategic moves by either team. A baseball umpire must know when to expect a sacrifice, a double steal, a squeeze play, a tag-up on a fly, or an attempt to nail the lead runner on a hit to the outfield. Basketball officials must sense a potential press, fast break, trap, or a strategic deliberate foul by the team that is behind in the score.

A team that is behind in the score in any sport may employ certain techniques to overcome that disadvantage, just as the team in front will strive to keep its lead. A losing volleyball team may increase its attempts to block spikes instead of simply trying for a defensive dig and subsequent set. A losing baseball team may try to pick runners off base or even block base paths while in the field. A winning football team may reduce its passing attempts and rely on ball control to keep the other team from coming back. In soccer or hockey, losing teams may abandon the net by pulling their own goalie and inserting an extra attack player in a desperate effort to score. A solid axiom of officiating asserts, "Anticipate the play, not the foul." Officials benefit from a knowledge of strategy that allows them to look for special tactics.

Spectators tend to watch the ball, but officials have to see both the movement of the ball and the actions of other players. In baseball, for example, outfielders must be observed retrieving a hit, runners must be observed to make sure they touch bases and do not run past teammates on the bases, and infielders must be observed to see whether they are placing themselves in the runners' paths. Umpires have to watch a lot of almost simultaneous action, and they have to watch the ball too, because the ball will take them to the spot where a judgment is necessary.

Almost any sport requires an official to view a wide range of simultaneous player action. Football may be the most problematic of all. At the snap, more than a dozen people at the line collide in an instant. Others are running pass routes, while defenders are backpedaling in pursuit and players in the offensive backfield are setting up to pass or trying to flee with the ball. It is important for officials to develop the habits of seeing a

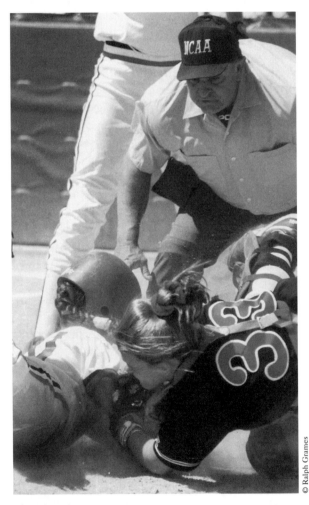

Anticipating a play means having a firm notion of what each opponent is attempting to accomplish. Here, Umpire Jim Gilbert knows what he's watching for and will be ready to make the right call.

© Ralph Grames

play unfold as a sequence of discrete, miniature actions and watching the potential receiver instead of the ball. This is called off-ball coverage, and the official must know his or her precise assignment, must hustle to be in a position to make the proper judgment, and must know the rights and restrictions of players to whom the ball is aimed.

Be in Proper Position

Along with sound judgment, the mechanics of positioning and moving with the action of the game are fundamental to the role of the sports official. As discussed in the previous section, an official's attention often must be focused on areas that spectators are not watching: potential recipients of the ball, for instance, or players who are moving so as to obstruct illegally. The official must learn how to select and react to the behavior of particular key players. Players readying themselves to block an attempted spike in volleyball, receivers running pass routes in football, rebounders vying for position under the rim in basketball, and fielders relaying outfield throws in baseball are all examples of vital player actions that may go unnoticed by spectators. Officials have to discard their spectator caps when working games.

To be at the proper spot to make correct calls, you have to read what teams are trying to do in games. You have to know how a fast break operates in basketball, for instance, and how teams attack a zone press and half-court trap. In football, you should be able to decipher the strengths of formations such as double wideouts, unbalanced lines, and shotgun setups. Baseball and softball infielders sometimes position themselves to cut off a key run, or the team at bat may bunt or try to "stretch" base runners in an attempt to force the defense into a mistake. Knowing how teams react to the score is a big asset. With knowledge of what a team is trying to do, an official can anticipate where the next call is likely to take place and what kind of action to expect. Judicious anticipation allows the official to move into the most advantageous position.

Each sport has its carefully detailed manual about reacting to the game: how to observe and

Do what it takes to get in position to make the call, and then be sure to make that call.

where to situate yourself to see things clearly. Knowledge and effective habits can also be learned from others (mentors, partners, association members, etc.) or in formal classes. You can also emulate officials in professional sports, even though you may not aspire to join their ranks. In televised games, close-ups of officials often reveal their facial expressions. They give a distinct impression of alertness without obvious signs of tension. Watch them run from one spot to the next. Their bursts of energy show hustle, a determination to be on top of things and to reach the right place at the right time. Notice them stop to observe a play. They seldom are comfortable making a critical decision while on the run. See how an NFL official obtains a runner's forward progress spot or an out-of-bounds designation. Persistent intensity when covering action and exceptional judgment are what elevate individuals to prominent positions. Compare the maneuvers of professionals with those of officials you watch at high school games. See whether they convey an impression of complete control—nothing hesitant, nothing frantic.

One way top-flight officials practice good tactics is to imagine scenarios in their minds, mentally creating game situations, particular phases that pose problems, problems in judgment and execution, and even problems with difficult people. All effective people—whether managers formulating an address to staff, engineers mulling the design of a structure, attorneys preparing to address a jury, or sports officials preparing for a game—use imaging, or inward rehearsing, to enhance their performance.

Despite the best preparation, even seasoned officials find themselves occasionally drawn to the wrong spots on the field or floor. Though professional officials are trained to engage all their senses, taking in the whole play and processing it briefly before making a decision, they unfortunately cannot slow a lightning blur of action, see action from various angles, or replay the action as television cameras can. Mistakes in college and professional officiating are often magnified and repeated by the media, and the prolonged criticism places tremendous pressure on officials at that level of broad exposure. If an official is out of position to make a call, he or she has two choices. One is to make the best "long-distance" call. The other choice is to rely on partners. Officials often have signals for communicating with partners when necessary, as discussed later in this chapter.

© Jeff Soucek / IHSA

Officials need to stay focused all the time, even when not observing a play directly. "Expect the unexpected" and "never be caught off guard" are vital slogans to live by.

Focus

Players focus on what they have to do to achieve success in a game. Officials must do the same thing. They have to know when game action sets up a critical decision. When the batter hits a ground ball and runners begin to move, the umpire knows that a decision is imminent at a base. Even when runners are obviously safe, the official has to be on top of the play to make the call. When bodies collide, officials must make an instant choice about the legality of the contact. "Ready or not, here I come," is what play action says to an official.

There are dead spots in every game when the temptation to let the mind wander is strong. Dead spots are opportunities to review the action so far, to assess the current game situation, and to analyze what is likely to happen next. Try to anticipate what strategy a coach will employ when play resumes. Dead spots should be opportunities for analysis of the game at hand.

Focus means concentration. Just as a superior athlete does, the official must focus on the game and shut out distractions. A wide variety of irrelevant distractions clamor for attention during a game, so an official must search for essential events throughout the game by adopting a narrow focus. Fatigue and overriding outside influences, such as sharp and prolonged criticism, may be obstacles to concentration. The official must push these aside to be effective.

Be Calm

Game action and people's responses to it can get hectic from time to time. When something unusual happens in a game, players, coaches, and spectators may become wild-eyed and unreasonable. At such times, an official must make a conscious effort to remain calm, to view the flurry dispassionately. The more furious play becomes, the more an official should adopt a cool, deliberate approach to ensure a clear vision of what is going on. Sometimes a calculated pause allows an official to process events more clearly. Though this seems to contradict the advice to keep a game moving, an outburst of fury or an exceptionally strange occurrence disrupts the tempo anyway. At these times, an official does not want to appear excited or emotionally wrought. In the midst of frenzied action, an official has to *work* to relax.

By measuring people's brain waves, psychologists have discovered that it is impossible to maintain a completely focused mental state at all times. The mind operating at maximum speed, as when all five senses are zeroed in on game action, can lead to sensory overload, which cannot be maintained for long periods. Such bursts of intense focus cause a person to experience anxiety and later drift into lethargy during a "swing" phase of recovery. A sports official operates more efficiently in an alert but not intense state of mind. The rate of brain wave activity can be controlled consciously by talking to oneself and programming one's reactions.

A deliberate slowing of the mental process can produce a level attitude. The term *level attitude* derives from the training of airline pilots: Keeping the wings level with the horizon in emergencies readily counters a force that interferes with flight. "Keeping the wings level" is a good image for sports officials to employ.

The best way to approach a game so that you remain alert but at ease is to use positive self-talk. Assure yourself that the experience is going to be enjoyable, that your decisions will be accepted in a spirit of wholesome competition, and that if problems arise, you are the catalyst who will solve them. "I'm in charge, but I will use a serene kind of game administration: not demonstrative, but quietly competent. I'll deal with every controversy with a level outlook."

Work With Fellow Officials

Often, you'll be paired with other officials when working games. There are sensible ways to get along. Fellow officials will usually tell you how they intend to operate, and they will in turn ask how you plan to work. This is not the time to be vague. Exchange honest points of view about positioning and techniques, and be accommodating. "I like to follow a dribbler from about 10 yards away, in a parallel position," a soccer ref may say. If that is different from what you are accustomed to, instead of insisting on a contrary method, try hard to adjust to your partner's preference. Inflexible officials tend to be mediocre, primarily because they are unable to accommodate the preferences of others.

The mechanics manual for each sport outlines the jurisdictions of particular officials at various points in games. In many geographic regions, special practices for dovetailing and sharing responsibilities have been adopted. For example, you need to know when to leave the infield as a base umpire to judge whether a fly ball or line drive has been trapped, muffed, or caught or has

© Jeff Soucek / IHSA

Each sport has areas that are especially demanding in terms of concentration and skill. A good way to test your accuracy and consistency is to have a fellow official observe and critique you during a game.

If You See It, Make the Call

When a plunge toward the goal occurs in football, customary responsibility for declaring a touchdown rests with the two side officials who are pledged to watch the penetration of the plane, that is, the ball being carried over the goal. But often a quarterback sneak-carries the ball into the end zone, and only the umpire observes it. The quarterback can actually be pushed back into the field of play after nudging the ball across the line. Even referees have seen runners twisted and thrust back after scoring a touchdown. Any official who sees a runner score is obligated to make the call if he or she is the only one to observe it.

cleared a fence. At the same time, you need to feel confident that a partner is covering for you as players run the bases.

Basketball officials have to rotate coverage, sliding across the floor in smooth synchrony. Football officials are assigned certain areas to observe contact, direction of attack, and pass routes. Sometimes jurisdictions overlap, meaning that more than one official can make a call in a given area. Sometimes the jurisdiction is not well defined, so officials have to notify one another during play action about how they are going to cover a specific area or play. Meshing duties with one another is an art. In some cases visual signals are used, but in other cases vocal cues are necessary. A football official can point to an eligible receiver whom he is going to watch at the snap. A softball or baseball umpire can call, "I've got the runner," on a long hit with the bases empty so that the base umpire knows to move toward home plate in case of overthrows. Players sometimes get in the way of officials, so other officials have to compensate. Officials must alert one another as necessary to help a crew member whose view may have been obscured or who may have fallen.

Although officials should follow recommended guidelines about their jurisdictions, those guidelines cannot be absolute. Any official who sees a play should call it, particularly if he or she was the only official to see it with certainty.

You should learn when to get and give help from other officials. It is not always politic to volunteer an opinion. Many officials have dug themselves into the proverbial hole by refusing to seek a partner's help, but just as many officials get themselves in trouble by saying the wrong thing at the wrong time. One practice that has filtered down from the professional level to the high school level is holding a conference to decide what is right when a question arises about a ruling.

Summary

Officiating requires complex decisions. These decisions, to be fair and accurate, require a deep knowledge of the sport, both technical knowledge of the rules and a feel for the spirit of the game. To make good calls, you must apply principles of fairness and not let unfair acts slip by. You must understand the rules, logic, terminology, and strategy of the game and know where, when, and how to make calls. You also need to know when to consult with or defer to other officials.

Because sport is *competition* and your decisions may sometimes be controversial, misunderstandings and disputes can arise. The next chapter offers ideas for resolving contentions that happen during a game.

6

Managing Conflict

Bill Topp

In this chapter you'll learn

- how conflict can result from misperceptions about officials,

- signs of potential conflict from game participants,

- the importance of having a conflict management plan, and

- how to implement your management plan.

"Please don't shoot the umpire: He is doing the best he can." A Kansas City baseball park posted that inscription on a sign in 1880 because of the proliferation of abusive baseball fans.

Conflict Is Inevitable

To manage conflict effectively, you must understand that conflicts are inevitable. Some commonplaces about conflict should be acknowledged right from the start. When two teams compete in a sports event, conflict is already present. It may be mild, it may be subdued, and it may even be masked by the appearance of harmony, but the potential for aggrieved feelings is always lurking. An event in the game may trigger an eruption, a series of difficulties may cause frustration to build, and sometimes decisions or nondecisions by officials make the officials themselves the focal point of anger.

As an official, you must approach any contest with the notion that a central part of the job requirement is handling conflict successfully. Although officials cannot gauge their success with a scoreboard, when conflict is managed well, officials can take a measure of satisfaction in their role.

A favorite slogan among officials is, "you've got to love it when they boo," because it is a fact that onlookers sometimes offer catcalls and sarcastic comments to officials. Coaches, players, and game administrators often show politeness, even deference, before a game begins, but once the contest starts, participants' and their followers' behavior can become snide, if not downright ugly.

As an objective participant who must make calls that affect either team, you won't be able to please people consistently. Therefore, your goal should not be to please people. You are there to arbitrate competition, and the most you can hope for is respect. Officiating is not a popularity contest.

The reasons why spectators and participants vent their anger at officials are complex and numerous. Exploring this issue shows that the problem does not always lie with the official. Understanding that may make the anger easier to forgive. We live in a society that insists on placing blame. Often blame is placed on officials unfairly. Keep that in mind as we explore ways to deal with conflicts.

Conflicts With Players' Parents

Officials are also sometimes blamed for other people's inadequacies. Parents may want to shift the blame for a player's lack of talent, a coaching strategy that misfires, or players' or coaches' responsibility for inadequate play. Other factors can be identified too: perceptions clouded by desire for a favorable judgment in a close play, general lack of respect for authority figures, and a warped sense of tradition that says it's all right to take it out on the officials.

Do you suppose a Little League parent has ever barked at an umpire to save face with neigh-

bors after his daughter struck out? to diminish the pressure on the child? in frustration with perceived inadequacies of the youngster? from impatience with his own lack of success in vicariously experiencing an athletic life he never had or failure to relive the athletic life he did have? to displace anger at a coach because the coach failed to teach the daughter properly or his own shame because he himself did not teach the daughter properly? from fury at a mother who forced the daughter into the sport? Frustration can be compounded by contextual factors, such as whether this was the girl's first at-bat of the season, whether her team was ahead or behind 26-0, or whether the game was close with the bases loaded in the last inning. Parents' frustrations when their children don't succeed are innumerable, and blaming the official is sometimes a convenient outlet.

Conflicts With Players

Players, too, sometimes react to officials negatively. Responsible players play the game and adjust to officials' styles, personalities, and abilities without complaining. They genuinely respect authority. However, some players—even

Understanding why players have conflicts with other players can help you deal with them calmly and effectively. Simply keeping players apart often reduces tensions.

professionals—blame officials (and teammates and coaches, too) for their own inabilities. Pat Swilling, former Oakland Raiders linebacker, commented on the Raiders' setting an NFL record for penalties: "I've heard [the officials] are out to get [Raiders' owner] Al Davis. I've never been on a team that's been penalized as much as we have. You see the penalties that people do to us and they're not called. Any little thing that we do is called." Those who blame others for their own shortcomings have a convenient excuse for failing. It is certainly easier on the psyche to make someone else the scapegoat than it is to accept responsibility for one's own actions.

Some high school players view sports officials as they view policemen or school authority figures. Rebellion is often a part of a child's growth process, especially in formative teen years. Rebellious kids like to break rules. Referees enforce rules. Conflict results.

Some players think opposing players get breaks from officials. The perception that your opponents are not judged by the same criteria as your team can make an official an easy target for criticism. Officials are only human, too, and it's possible that an official's honest mistake can be perceived as bias.

Conflicts With Coaches

Coaches can also be antagonistic. "A coach spends his entire life thinking he's fighting off alligators. A referee is just another alligator," said Jack Pardee, former Houston Oilers football coach.

Coaches and officials can have an adversarial relationship because of one major factor: Coaches care who wins and referees don't. Because coaches are pulling for their team, devising offensive and defensive strategies, and keeping a keen eye on their individual players, they see the game with a built-in bias. They want things to go their way, and they will events to go in their favor. As a consequence, they are sometimes quick to view officials' decisions as unfair. They may sometimes feel that they have to fight the officials as well as their opponents. Some rare coaches even view their role as a contriver or antagonist in relation to officials. They may howl, whine, and plead in an effort to gain a presumed edge from officials.

Some coaches contend that officials aren't accountable. Coaches can get fired if they don't win. They see officials as having no one to answer to when a call is wrong. This is a typical lament from a frustrated coach: "If I foul up, I could lose my job. If an official goofs, the league says they're sorry, and the official keeps the job. Sanctions and reprimands should result from bad calls." Although officials sometimes are subject to dismissal or dropped from leagues due to perceived shortcomings, many coaches are unaware of this.

Coaches often do whatever it takes to gain a mental edge for victory. Some coaches purposely behave in a way that irritates officials, believing that such antics will somehow work to their advantage. Coaches may manipulate situations to make themselves look good or to incite their players. It's not uncommon for coaches to try to get ejected for motivational and theatrical purposes.

Coaches sometimes use the officials as scapegoats as a means of inspiring their players. It's not unusual for a coach deliberately to attempt to be warned or even ejected by an official in hopes of igniting the players.

Sometimes officials become pawns that a coach uses to fuel the emotions of players and fans.

The home team, a clear favorite, is losing and playing poorly in front of a large crowd. The umpire makes a close but correct call, and a home team player is out. The coach storms out of the dugout to confront the umpire and says, with arms flailing, "That was a close call, and I think you got it right. I'm out here to get those fans in the game and get my team going. You made the right call, but I want my players to think I'm out here fighting for them." The coach ends the "argument" and goes back into the dugout. The home team rallies from behind to win the game.

Some coaches believe that officials are influenced by the officials' own expectations. For instance, if a team has a reputation for superior play and a winning record, the coaches may believe that the team will receive soft or tolerant treatment by officials because the officials expect a top-flight performance. Conversely, if a team's or coach's reputation is such that officials anticipate sloppy or dirty play or a lackadaisical or belligerent attitude, the coaches may expect officials to respond to the reputation rather than the actual behavior. "Expect trouble and you get trouble," one saying holds.

Many coaches try to gain an advantage any way they can to win, including intimidating or begging officials in the hope that the next call goes in their favor. Some coaches resort to being manipulative, and every phrase uttered to an official before and during a contest has a calculated purpose. Humans are prone to be influenced by propaganda and flattery. Watch how TV commercials and print ads act as sales devices. Many coaches have adopted the same persuasive techniques and are effective salespeople for their teams.

Whether these psychological tactics work or not, officials must deal with them. When coaches yell about a particular call, they almost invariably know that the official is not going to change that call. They may think, however, that making a scene about that call will plant seeds of doubt in an official's head and work to their advantage later.

Conflicts With Administrators

Athletic administrators can be dismissive of officials. "For years people have looked on umpiring as a job they could get any postman to do. In fact, Joe Cronin (once American League president) was having an argument during a meeting with the umpires. He told them, 'You guys better look at this,' and pulled out all the applications and a list of the umpires who had written to him. He said, 'I can get 24 postmen to replace you guys.' That's really the way they sometimes feel about you," said Doug Harvey, retired National League umpire.

Athletic directors may be officials' biggest supporters or worst detractors. Officials need the support of game administrators from time to time for securing dressing facilities, handling equipment adjustments at the game, controlling spectators, arranging game assistants (scorekeepers, ball chasers, timers, chain crews, etc.), and providing postgame escorts after controversial contests. Administrators may or may not be conscientious and efficient in these duties. When they are deficient, officials themselves may have to solve problems that arise. Poor game administrators can be notable by their absence.

Administrators at all levels know that officials are necessary to conduct a contest, but there are likely more problems related to officiating than any other aspect of their job. For example, scheduling officials is time-consuming, finding last-minute replacement officials is troublesome, listening to complaints from coaches and fans about officials' perceived inabilities is tiresome, and justifying expenses for officials is sometimes difficult when dealing with budget-conscious school boards.

Recognizing Conflict

You can't manage a conflict if you don't recognize clues to volatile emotions. Some conflicts are easy to recognize; others are more subtle. Learning to recognize signs of conflict—whether it is two opponents swinging at each other or clues that a player or coach is about to explode in unsportsmanlike conduct—can help you deal with a conflict before it escalates. When you read the signs correctly, you can prevent major blowups.

Signs From Players

Frustrated players tend to complain or demonstrate nonverbal signs of disgust. Knowing the signs of frustration gives you the context to deal with the player appropriately.

■ A player's poor performance is an obvious sign of a player's frustration level. If a player is playing well, you're less likely to hear complaining. If a star player is struggling, you'll hear more complaining.

■ Look at players' facial expressions and body language for clues about their feelings. Staring or glaring at an opponent is an obvious attempt at intimidation. Tense facial muscles, such as a set jaw, may indicate that a player is close to acting aggressively. Players who scold teammates are usually frustrated also.

■ Always watch for contact away from the ball or after a play ends, including after tags in baseball and softball. Because of the perception that no one is watching in those two situations, players may execute a verbal or physical cheap shot.

■ Be on constant lookout for "paybacks." For example, after a hard foul, look for the offended player to attempt to get the fouling player back at some point. Some players attempt to retaliate immediately; they are often caught because the officials are still focused on them. Sneakier players try to retaliate later, hoping the referees aren't watching anymore.

Signs From Coaches

When coaches' comments to officials are repetitive, it is usually a sign of either frustration or an attempt to manipulate the officials. The volume of their comments is also a sign. Watch for sudden, aggressive body language, too.

■ Look for how they talk to their own players and assistant coaches. If they're haranguing them, the officials may also be a target at some point.

■ Body language is crucial. Look for stern facial expressions that express anger or a roll of the eyes and a wry smile that suggests sarcasm. A coach flailing arms or using officiating signals is a sure sign that the coach is playing to the crowd in an attempt to intimidate you.

Planning for Conflict: Using Preventive Officiating

Part of being a good official is being a strategist. Just like successful people in any endeavor, good

officials have a game plan. Getting ready for a game usually involves a pregame conference with partners. The majority of pregame conferences focus on rules, mechanics, court coverage, and foul-calling philosophy. Rarely discussed but equally important is a conflict management game plan.

The best conflict management plans include preventive officiating. In fact, most of your efforts in conflict management should be focused on preventing conflict from escalating. If you can stop a potentially bad situation from developing, there's less conflict to deal with. This should be your main goal in conflict management. Following are some basic techniques that can help prevent conflict from arising or escalating further.

Clear Your Head

One of your first challenges is to forget temporarily other parts of your life before the game. When you've had a stressful day, it is imperative to shelve your problems while you officiate your game. You have a duty to the game and its participants to be ready to officiate. Many people enjoy officiating because it gives them the chance to forget about everything else for awhile.

Know Your Participants

Part of a good conflict management plan is gaining knowledge about participants. There is a fine line between preparation and prejudice. On the surface it would seem that the more information you have, the better prepared you will be. The dangerous flip side is letting the information you've gathered negatively influence the way you handle a situation. The following example shows how information can help; the example in the section after that shows how it can hurt.

You've been assigned to referee a football game between crosstown rivals. Because you're familiar with the history of the rivalry, you know there's been trouble between the two in the past. The teams and coaches don't like each other. Based on that history, you correctly assume that there's likely to be a lot of emotion in the game, probably more than a typical game. You've heard through the officiating grapevine that last year when the teams played, a bench-clearing brawl erupted, and threats of payback were often heard.

As an official, you want that type of information. You're less likely to be surprised by unseemly events. You want to be prepared for bad blood between teams in every game you work, and having detailed information helps you and your crew focus on potential problems before they happen.

In a situation like the one in this example, you may need to deal with things differently than you would in a less hostile situation. For example, a playful jibe by a player to an opponent in a normal setting might not get a strong reaction. Officials might use preventive officiating by talking to the player who made the comment to make sure it doesn't happen again. That same comment in an emotion-filled game might draw a more volatile reaction from an opponent. The official should understand the context and deal with the problem more sternly, using stronger language or even penalizing without warning if necessary to control the situation.

Stay Objective

Having good information before a game gives you the proper context to handle things appropriately for that game, but sometimes prior information can sway your opinion if you don't make objectivity your goal. Here's a situation where information negatively prejudices an official:

Through the officiating grapevine, you hear stories from other refs about how basketball coach John Doe at Anywhere High School is extremely difficult. According to the officials, Coach Doe is mean and is constantly berating officials. "I ejected the coach last year," you hear from one ref. Another says, "I should've this year. If I ever see him again, I'm going to get it done this time."

You're assigned to officiate at Anywhere High School a week after you've heard those comments. You've never had a game with that coach before. In the first minute of the game, Coach Doe shouts, "Traveling!" after an opponent makes a move to the basket. Without hesitation, you call a technical foul on Coach Doe and say, "You're not going to intimidate me tonight. Don't even think of trying it!" The coach's comment did not deserve a penalty—it did not even deserve a response. Clearly, because of the negative information gathered before the game, you have become biased against the coach. You overreacted because of your expectations. Knowing beforehand of Coach Doe's bad reputation is not the problem; the problem is letting that information influence your judgment.

Processing the knowledge gained about a particular team, player, coach, or game calls for careful judgment. Gain enough information to help you understand why certain things are happening in the game. Be responsible enough to sort through the information and treat each game as a new one.

Don't Take It Personally

A coach tells you, "Shake your head, your eyes are stuck. You're terrible. If you had one more eye you'd be a cyclops." As an official, you have to deal with such comments but not take them personally. One of the most difficult aspects to understand about officiating is that generally when people yell at you, they're really yelling at your official's uniform and what it represents. When you're challenged by anyone involved in the game, there's a good chance that the victim could have been any official who happened to be there. That doesn't make it right, but knowing ahead of time that the challenge is not personal will help you deal with it better.

No matter how well you do in officiating, some people will vent their frustrations on you. Coaches, players, and fans have an intensely personal interest in games, which means that their judgment tends to be impaired and their comments suspect. Understand and accept that participants are going to see things differently than you do. An old officiating saying goes, "Coaches, players, and fans see the game with their hearts. Refs see the game with their eyes." That wisdom should be applied to both negative and positive comments. Winning coaches, simply because they've won, are perhaps more likely than losing coaches to feel that the officials have done a decent job. If you believe them when they tell you that you're good, you better also believe them when they tell you that you're bad.

Decide What Deserves a Response

Part of your management plan must include when you're going to respond to people. You are going to be challenged in varying degrees. Every question does not need a response. Statements require no answer. Realize that coaches and players are often simply venting their frustrations when chal-

Referee Dave Habeb gets some unsolicited help from a coach during a high school game. The dual listening/ignoring charade is part of the gamesmanship of sports.

lenging you. Always decide whether to respond before you start responding. This is difficult to do in a heated situation, but if you take that moment to think before speaking, you can prevent a conflict from escalating.

> If a basketball coach says, "She's camping in the lane," what is more effective: ignoring the statement or saying to the coach, "No way; she's been fine all night"? Most of the time, ignoring a harmless statement or acknowledging it with a simple head nod ends the matter. When you defend your position, the coach instinctively may go on the offensive and continue the debate. Ask yourself, "If I say something, will it do more harm than good?"

Understand Game Context

The intensity of the game, the closeness of the score, and the time left in the game all play a part in how much and what type of conflict you must deal with. With a close score at the end of a game—no matter the sport or level—emotions rise. A foul called in the early stages of the game may draw few complaints from players, coaches, and fans. A similar foul call in the final moments of a tight game will likely elicit a more emotional response from all involved. Consider allowing the participants a bit more leeway in such situations.

That doesn't mean you should let a player or coach get away with extremely unsportsmanlike conduct simply because the score is close at the end of a game. It does mean, however, that the way you handle that end-of-game situation will likely have great impact on the result, so you should consider the emotional charge of the situation and tolerate a bit more than you normally would in less critical situations.

Implementing Your Conflict Management Plan

During each game, you must recognize the signs of conflict, prevent it from escalating, and deal directly with it by penalizing when appropriate. How officials handle each of those elements separates average officials from exceptional ones.

Conflict Management Tools

Looking as if you know what you're doing and are confident in your handling of situations goes a long way toward managing conflict. Physical presence, voice control, body language, and whistle or flag usage are vital conflict management tools.

Your Presence

Marshall McLuhan, known as the "father of advertising," suggested that how you do something is sometimes more important than what you do. Officials must sell calls effectively. Presence is a selling tool for officials.

Presence is difficult to define. An official with presence looks athletic and has a confident demeanor that says, "I belong." An official without presence often looks nervous and appears to be anxious. Coaches can sense a lack of confidence and may become aggressive, thinking that they can easily influence that official to gain an advantage.

Younger officials should be prepared to deal with more conflict than older officials. Coaches tend to test rookies because they believe that rookies are more easily influenced than veterans. Although age is a factor that you can't control, young officials can be well prepared by thinking about what they are going to say before they say it.

Good officials look good. They are physically fit and appear athletic. They walk confidently with a strong posture. How does that relate to managing conflict? The more authoritative you look, the more accepting people are. The more accepting people are, the less conflict you'll have to manage.

Your physical presence also means where you are in relation to the conflict. Sometimes you can defuse a problematic situation merely by being in the same physical location.

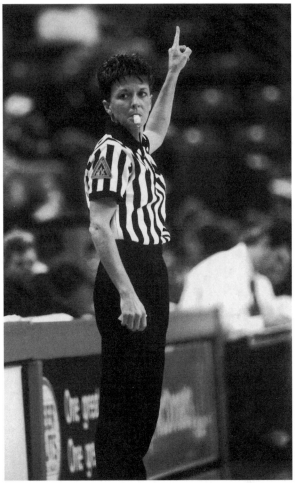

Your physical presence affects the way others perceive you. If you look strong and confident, your calls may not be questioned as often.

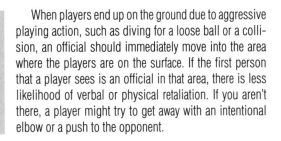

When players end up on the ground due to aggressive playing action, such as diving for a loose ball or a collision, an official should immediately move into the area where the players are on the surface. If the first person that a player sees is an official in that area, there is less likelihood of verbal or physical retaliation. If you aren't there, a player might try to get away with an intentional elbow or a push to the opponent.

Your Voice

The way you talk to a person has a tremendous impact on the response you receive. At times, an official's inappropriate reply causes a conflict with a coach or player. As officials, we have to ask ourselves the extent to which we are the problem. Officials should never indulge in verbal retaliation. Remember to use the good communication and listening skills discussed in chapter 4.

Be firm, loud enough to be heard, but not challenging. Your voice can be a positive tool that helps you control a game, or it can be a dagger used to hurt a perceived opponent. Remember, the more you say in a situation of conflict, the less it means. In many cases, deciding not to say anything is the best way to use your voice.

Keep Emotion out of Your Voice. Use your voice to defuse situations, not add emotion to them. What is a person's first reaction to a barked order? During a conflict, he or she may become defiant, tense his or her muscles, and yell back.

It's a natural defense mechanism. Consequently, when an official barks at a player or coach, the player's or coach's first instinct is to snap back. Although he or she may not reply defiantly right away to avoid a penalty, the player or coach may store that anger. It will likely surface later, and officials want to avoid that.

Avoid Threats. Officials' ultimatums back the officials themselves into corners as much as coaches and players. Many officials have used the phrase, "One more word and you're gone!" Most officials who repeatedly use the "one more word" threat fail to understand its ramifications. How literally should you interpret that threat? For example, if the coach responds, "You're an over-officious jerk," the coach has clearly gone too far; you have no choice but to penalize. But what if the coach replies, "You're right. I apologize. I'll just coach my team from now on"? Because the coach did say "one more word," would you penalize just to keep your word or accept the apology and back down from your threat? Getting backed into such corners is a problem with using threats. Instead of using threatening words, use phrases such as, "I've heard enough." That's far less provocative, doesn't carry an ultimatum that may have unintended consequences, yet gets your message across.

Point to a Shared Goal. If you need to address something that a player or coach is doing—before assessing a penalty if you use preventive officiating—keep the common goal in mind. Here's an example: "Coach, we need to work together to ensure the safety of all players. Can you please talk to number 45 about the rough play out here? That will help us protect the players. Thank you." By letting the coach know that you both have a common goal—in this case, protecting the players—you're more likely to get cooperation from the coach.

Don't Argue. One obvious way to avoid an argument is not to get drawn into the argument. When a coach wants to argue, don't respond in kind. Simply state, "When we can talk to each other instead of screaming, I'll enter the conversation." Avoid aggressive body language, and talk calmly and slowly to lower the emotion of the conversation. It's not an argument if you don't participate!

Tell the Truth. It's okay to say you made a mistake. Honesty is your best policy. Under no circumstances should you try to lie your way out of trouble. Others know or will find out, and they'll think you can't be trusted. Lying fuels negative perceptions of officials.

An old school of thought in officiating was, "Never admit to making a mistake." That philosophy has gone away. If you blew a call, it's okay to admit it quietly to the coach or player. Many times, they'll respect you more for your honesty than if you tried to twist the truth and equivocate. Most coaches understand that you can't change judgment calls, but admitting you messed up often ends the argument. If you do it too often, however, your reputation will suffer.

Don't Trivialize. Though extremely tempting sometimes, don't ever utter the phrase, "It's just a game." Few phrases enrage participants more quickly than that one. Remember, they've worked all week, all season, and all their careers for that game. It is critically important to them, no matter what the sport or level. That phrase is often interpreted by coaches and players as flippant, uncaring, and demeaning.

Your Body Language

When a player or coach challenges you, consider what your body language says to observers. Avoid crossing your arms in front of your chest. That movement appears too aggressive. Also avoid an aggressive hands-on-hips stance with your chest thrust out. When an argument ensues, consider placing your hands behind your back. Stand tall and strong while doing so. That stance does not appear confrontational yet shows you're in control. At all times, avoid pointing at a player or coach. That gesture appears too aggressive and almost always gets a heated response, such as, "Get your finger out of my face!" Make solid eye contact during the discussion. If your eyes wander looking elsewhere or your head moves around, it appears that you're either intimidated by the coach or not sure of your position. Neither is good for the conversation. Also try hard not to scowl.

From the moment you arrive at the game site, you're on stage in effect. Think about what you would look like if you were on TV and there were no sound. Constantly ask yourself, "What does

College umpire Lyall Boudreaux seems to be saying, "Hold it. I want to make a point."

this look like?" By doing so, you'll remember to use body language that sends positive signals and avoids confrontational movements and gestures. As a result, your challenges will decrease.

Here's a situation illustrating how body language alone can escalate a conflict.

As a high school softball umpire, you call a runner out on a close play at second base. The coach comes out of the dugout and onto the field to ask you about the call. Early in the exchange, the coach is calm and talking in relatively normal tones. The coach simply wants an explanation of the call: "I know you were closer to the play than I was, but it looked to me as if my player was in there. What did you see on the play?"

While the coach is talking, you don't say anything verbally, but your body language shows you're not pleased with the coach. You strongly fold your arms in front of your chest, have a smirk on your face, and then roll your eyes.

Watching your body language, the coach becomes agitated and says, "Hey, I'm just out here asking a ques-

tion, and I have a right to do that. I've shown you respect, and I expect the same from you." With that, you raise your hand up as a stop signal, then dismissingly wave the coach back to the bench, all with a cocky smile on your face.

The coach gets closer to you, stands firm, and yells, "You've got an attitude problem! You're not bigger than the game. I'm going to send a report to the high school state office." You then eject the coach.

Throughout the scenario, you didn't say a single word, yet your body language screamed at the coach a variety of negative messages, including disrespect, arrogance, and an unwillingness to listen. Better body language (eye contact, a comfortable stance with hands behind your back, a nod to let the coach know you understood the concern) coupled with a solid verbal explanation would have helped you address the coach professionally and avoid a heated argument.

Your Whistle or Flag

Your whistle and your flag are also communication tools. Think of them as an extension of your voice. When you blow a weak whistle, you're more likely to be challenged because it sounds as though you're not sure of yourself. Conversely, an overly loud whistle equates to screeching. There are times when you need a loud whistle (to get a person's attention, in a loud setting, to help sell a call, etc.), but constantly blowing your whistle as loudly as you can is like yelling every call. Blow a strong, steady whistle with normal volume in most situations. If the situation requires you to be a bit louder and firmer, blow your whistle a bit harder, but use that tone sparingly. Don't use short, repetitive blasts except to get someone's attention in a loud setting because they draw unnecessary attention to you and can be perceived as overaggressiveness or hostility to the offender.

The same principles apply to use of the flag by football and soccer officials. Your flag is a method of communicating. In football, if you throw a weak flag that looks as if it simply fell out of your pocket, it suggests that you're unsure about your call. Slamming an angry flag into the ground equates to screaming; you appear to have lost control and are belittling the offender. Throw the flag on an arc so that it flies gracefully through the air toward the area of the foul and doesn't look as if you're throwing it aggressively at someone. Similarly, if an assistant soccer referee's flag is raised slowly or at "half mast," the referee looks unsure of the call. Extend the flag in an even line directly from your shoulder to the tip of the flag.

Team Captains

The team captain is an often underutilized yet critically important game management tool for officials. A good relationship with a captain gives you another way to handle players and coaches. To use the captain effectively, you must understand what captains are supposed to do and how they usually think.

The captain is a player whose duties include communicating with the officials. Pregame formalities and duties, such as going over ground rules, the coin toss, and so on, are often performed with captains. The captain serves as team spokesperson and acts as a liaison between the officials and the team's players and coaches. The captain is generally expected to have a leadership role on the team.

Sometimes the person selected as captain is not the real team leader. Despite a player's appointment or promotion to captain, another player may in fact be the team leader, especially if the appointment rotates. As an official, you want to find and work with the team leader, even if that leader is not the designated captain. Watch the teams during warm-ups and early in the game. Which player has the most influence on the team? Who does the team look to for answers when the coach is not around? If there's more than one captain on a team, have them designate one as the lead spokesperson. You don't want three or four captains asking questions throughout the game; one can handle it.

Use captains to your advantage. Ask them pertinent game-related questions or ask them to deal with minor game management duties. Let the captain have the first chance to a player who is getting out of line but deserves a warning and not a penalty. During dead time, say something like, "Captain, number 24 is starting to talk a bit to the opponent. Could you please handle that?" A good leader will quiet the offending player immediately. If that happens, thank the captain. Most captains take their roles very seriously. If you communicate with them and give them an

opportunity to be leaders, they can help you do your job.

Resolving Conflict

When you are involved in a conflict, your goal as an official is to resolve it. You have to fight the tendency to want to win the argument. The difference between resolving a conflict and winning it is critical to conflict management.

When resolving a conflict, the best outcome is when everyone "wins." If there is only one winner, the loser's self-esteem and trust are eroded. To avoid that, strive to have an open dialog and think about the words you choose and the way they affect the situation. There's an old officiating saying that summarizes this philosophy: "As officials, we always have the last word. However, we don't always have to say it."

In a *Referee* magazine feature story titled "Count to Ten," psychologist Dr. Bruce Baldwin detailed a plan to help resolve conflict:

1. *Permit the other person to talk without interrupting.* Have the courtesy to listen before you say anything. The other person is then more likely to extend you the same courtesy. When both sides have been adequately heard, problem solving begins.

Retired National League umpire Doug Harvey, one of the most respected officials ever to work in the profession, applied his "10-second rule." He gave a manager who argued with him 10 seconds to vent before responding. His theory was that the comments from the arguer were so emotional that his breath couldn't last for more than 10 seconds. When he stopped to take a breath, Harvey could calmly begin his explanation.

2. *Limit discussion only to the immediate issue that is adversely affecting your relationship.* One of the fastest ways to get off to a bad start in solving a problem is to rehash the past or bring other impertinent issues into the discussion, as a few coaches like to do. You must "keep them in the box," that is, keep them focused on the play or situation at hand. Coaches may try to talk about things that happened earlier in the game. When they do that, say something like, "Let's focus on this play and get it resolved. Now, how did you see this play?"

3. *Choose an optimal time to bring up and discuss problems.* Many problems that compromise positive conflict resolution can be avoided by carefully choosing the time to discuss a particular issue. To find that time, approach the other person when you are both calm and free to talk. Dead-ball time, such as a time-out or between periods, is a great time for officials to talk to people. Keep the conversations focused and brief.

4. *Judiciously avoid the other person's vulnerabilities or emotional sensitivities.* Everyone has personal vulnerabilities, and it's tempting to hit below the belt. It is a sign of maturity to avoid sensitive areas when engaged in conflict. A deliberate strike at a personal vulnerability is irrelevant as well as hurtful. It also invites a counterattack that focuses on your areas of sensitivity. No one will trust you with emotionally sensitive information if you use it as a weapon whenever there is a problem. In other words, it is inappropriate for the official to counterattack. A testy softball umpire once shouted to a coach who had questioned a call, "I see that white hair under your cap. You probably think your huge experience entitles you to second guess." Sarcasm is never a good instrument for promoting conflict resolution.

Probably the biggest temptation to avoid is using a team's record or game score as a weapon. When a team is losing by a large margin and a coach or player is complaining about a call, it is very tempting to fire back with, "You've won only three games this year, and you're way behind today. Maybe you should start focusing on playing instead of officiating. You've got a lot of work to do." Even if this is true, saying it is using a team's vulnerability to your advantage, which is a conflict management taboo.

5. *Regularly touch base with the other person.* It is customary not to take the time to talk when things seem to be going well. If you don't talk when things are going well, then angry interactions may be the only times when you have contact with coaches and players. Make it a point to comment periodically on the progress of the game, even if those remarks are trivial. Ongoing dialog is one of the best possible ways to avoid problems, but this can be difficult for officials because they can't have a constant running dialog with participants. Conversation should be limited to a few words at appropriate times, such as during a dead-ball interval. You should send the message that you are willing to communicate, not that you are commenting on all facets of play.

Tricks of the Trade

Preventive officiating is an important step in managing conflict. There are a number of tips and tricks that you can use to get your point across to players and coaches before penalizing them.

Use Your Lineup Card

In baseball or softball, if you need to talk to a coach about a problem, pull out your lineup card between innings before approaching the coach. While both of you look at the lineup card, make your point carefully yet firmly. The lineup card technique allows you to address a problem directly but discreetly, because everyone else in the ballpark thinks you're talking about something involving the lineup. You've accomplished what you wanted without embarrassing or challenging the coach in front of players or other observers.

Wipe the Ball

Anytime players sweat, they give you a conflict management tool. When a participant is causing problems in the game, use the "wipe the ball" technique to start a discreet discussion. During a dead ball—for example, when a basketball goes out of bounds—ask the nearest bench assistant for a towel to wipe the ball. While wiping off the ball, approach the problem participants and give your warning. Baseball umpires can accomplish the same thing by wiping off the plate. You can send the message unobtrusively while most people in the gym think you're simply doing routine cleaning.

Talk to Your Partner

Talk to your partner so players can hear. For example, during a dead ball, in a normal, unthreatening tone, tell your partner in front of the players, "Joe, number 4 for blue and 5 for white are starting to talk a bit too much to each other. Let's keep an eye on them." You've sent

Referee Jerry Stone asks cheerleaders to move away from the court to prevent a player from being injured. Heading off problems before they occur is "preventive officiating."

the message without directly confronting the players, a good preventive technique in the early stages of the problem.

Make a Deal

"He's holding!" One of the more consistent complaints from football linemen is that the opponent is holding. When you've decided the complaint needs to be addressed, make a deal with complainant, for example, "Okay, number 76. I've heard you. I'm going to watch you exclusively for the next three plays. If he doesn't hold you in the next three plays, the complaining stops." The player will almost always accept the conditions. If the complaint is true, call it. If not, gently tell the complaining player so: "He looked clean on those plays." More often than not, the player will return to playing and stop complaining.

Preventing Fights

When a fight erupts in a game, the officials may be held accountable—which can be damaging to their reputations and sometimes can result in

Put the Ball in Play

One of the most effective "tricks" really isn't a trick at all. When someone starts to complain, get the ball back in play as soon as possible. There is generally more complaining during dead-ball time than when the game is going on. Players have to play when the ball is live, and they won't have time to argue. Coaches also tend to get back to coaching when the ball is in play. Don't rush to the point of looking hurried, but get the ball back in play as soon as possible after a dead ball. Your conflicts will decrease.

legal action. It's hard for even the most competent and respected officials to bounce back from being labeled as someone who can't control a tough game. The best way to handle a fight is to prevent it from starting.

Know the Background

As previously discussed, information about the participants and possible rivalries can help prevent conflicts. To learn participants' history, talk to other officials. Share with other officials how and why fights that you've had to deal with took place.

In extreme situations, caution players and coaches before the game as a reminder that the officials are aware of potential problems. It's okay to let them think that you're going to call the game more tightly or be tougher on them but then call in your normal style. When addressing players or coaches before the game, end with a positive thought. Assure them that if they play the game the way it's meant to be played, there won't be any problems and that you will do everything you can to protect them and prevent conflicts from escalating.

Read the Signs

To prevent a fight successfully, you must pick up on the little signs that a bigger problem is imminent. The most obvious signs are verbal—trash talking or any type of intimidating or threatening words designed to embarrass or incite the opponent. Remember to watch participants' body language as discussed earlier for signs of anger or frustration.

Be Prepared

Prepare for the worst. That doesn't mean overreacting; it means knowing what you will do if certain things happen. Talk with your partners about team history and chemistry before every game. Map out your preventive plan of action. Discuss what you will do if a fight breaks out. By talking about potential problems with partners, you will be better prepared and more confident of how to handle even the worst situation if it arises.

Learn From It

If a fight does break out, learn from it. Think about what led up to the fight, which may reveal what you might have done to prevent it. Few

fights explode out of nowhere. You may have missed some signs at the time. By taking the time to review, you won't miss them again. Don't blame yourself. Coaches, administrators, and players must accept responsibility too.

When to Penalize

Preventive officiating means using informal warnings when possible and appropriate before a problem requires more severe action. The rules of many sports stipulate when formal warnings or penalties should be issued for specific infractions. Good officials must know these rules thoroughly and must also know how much leeway to grant participants.

What to Tolerate From Whom

It seems that officials get abuse from just about everyone present at a game, from spectators to players. Officials should tolerate different levels of abuse from different participants in the game. Though each official draws individual boundaries, the following sections offer guidelines for how much or little you should tolerate from a particular group. Remember, no extremely unsportsmanlike conduct should be tolerated from anyone.

Fans

Be more tolerant of fans than any other group. They've often paid money to root for their team, and some believe that includes the right to boo the officials. Never talk back to fans. Doing so only increases their abuse. At higher levels of play, tolerate more from fans than you would at lower levels of play. For example, a fan using profanity at a youth game shouldn't be tolerated, but fans using profanity at professional games are ignored by the officials. If a fan is using profanity or offensive terms at a youth game, have the fan removed from the premises immediately. Following is the proper method for doing this:

▮ Do not say anything to the fan.

▮ Stop the game, then approach the game administrator (or the home head coach if an administrator is not present), and explain that a particular fan is to be ejected for using improper language.

■ Let the game administrator handle the ejection. It's not your job to escort fans from the premises, except in some youth leagues where a policy may place responsibility for crowd behavior on the officials.

■ Delay the game until the problem is rectified. It might be appropriate to send players to their benches during the interruption.

At higher levels of play, it has become trendy for fans to throw coins and small objects on the floor. You should have game administrators warn or remove fans who throw objects on the floor. Fans who throw objects directly at an official or a player should be ejected immediately by the game administrator. If the offender can't be found in the crowd, suggest that the game administrator remove the fans from the section from which objects were thrown. Though you usually should be most tolerant with fans, you should have no tolerance for threats to players' or officials' safety.

Head Coaches

Because of the nature of their job, some head coaches create problems for officials. Use preventive officiating whenever you can, and tolerate a bit more from them than you would other participants.

As discussed earlier, coaches sometimes engage in manipulative behavior or grandstanding to gain a psychological advantage. One school of thought says if you know a coach is deliberately trying to get a penalty or ejection, you should ignore the antics and avoid being taken advantage of, but that rarely works. If a basketball coach whose team is down by 30 points wants to get the crowd fired up by running onto the court and blaming you, there's not much you can do but penalize the offender. If you don't penalize the actions, the coach will likely do something more severe until he or she is satisfied.

It's not easy to handle a manipulative coach. Here are some practical tips:

■ Game context dictates when a coach is most likely to use an official for motivational purposes. Time of game, score, and setting are all factors.

When a team is playing poorly at home, a coach is more likely to use an official to draw the crowd and the team into the game. Conversely, some coaches playing in a hostile environment may "buy a penalty" to turn the crowd against that coach's team and reinforce a feeling of "us against the world" in the players. Be aware of the situation, but don't let it dictate how you work the game.

■ Take care of business while maintaining an even keel. "Rewarding" a coach with a technical foul or ejection can test an official's emotional maturity. A good official administers the penalty without losing his or her cool and continues concentrating on the game.

■ Avoid engaging in a war of wills with a coach who's looking to manipulate you, the crowd, or the team. It may be tempting to be stubborn ("You can't make me throw you out. If I have to suffer through this, you do too"), but that attitude can backfire. If you let a coach get away with unsportsmanlike behavior, the coach of the other team will likely follow suit.

Starting Players

Starting players should get a bit more leeway than reserves, because that's who the fans come to see. While that doesn't give starting players free reign to abuse officials, it does mean that officials should use preventive officiating as much as possible to keep them in the game. If preventive officiating fails, penalize.

Assistant Coaches

Assistant coaches should get some leeway when they are complaining, but not much. It is an official's job to hear complaints from a head coach, not to deal with complaints from assistants.

Conflicts with assistants tend to heat up faster than conflicts with head coaches for a number of reasons. Officials expect complaints from head coaches. Dealing with a head coach's complaints one-on-one is less stressful than when two or three assistants chime in, which can make the official feel outnumbered. Many assistants are young; sometimes it's their first coaching job. Assistants may get less respect from older officials simply because they haven't been coaching long. Younger and less experienced coaches tend to be more emotional.

Here is how to handle assistant coaches:

■ Don't stereotype. It's not fair for officials to think all assistant coaches are trouble.

■ Don't treat assistants as inferiors. Today's assistant may be tomorrow's head coach.

■ Introduce yourself to the assistant before the game. A brief, polite meeting starts the communication positively.

■ Use an assistant to help manage the game. For example, the NFL and college football leagues have instituted an informal "get-back" coach, an assistant who is in charge of helping keep players in the team box and off the field.

■ Address problems with assistant coaches by talking to the head coach. In most cases, the head coach will squelch the assistant. The last thing a head coach wants is a penalty because of an assistant.

Bench Personnel

Other people on the bench (reserve players, trainers, team managers, etc.) should receive minimal tolerance. They each have a job to do that does not include commenting on the officiating. Address problems with bench personnel directly with the head coach. Often the coach will support you to avoid a penalty caused by other bench personnel.

Game Attendants

Often, scorers and timers are from the home school. Some can get caught up being fans and may create problems for officials. Remind attendants before the game that they are an important part of the officiating team and that neutrality is important. Most of the time you won't have problems. However, when a game attendant makes unnecessary comments or improper gestures, take care of it immediately. You can deal with the offender directly or preferably ask the game administrator to handle the problem. If you deal with it on your own, remind the offender that he or she is a part of the officiating team and that being a fan while in that role is inappropriate. If

improper conduct continues, have the game administrator remove the offender immediately.

Cheerleaders and Mascots

Cheerleaders and mascots should get close to zero tolerance. If you see a cheerleader incite the crowd against the officials or the opponents, deal with it immediately. Cheerleaders are not fans and should not be given as much leeway. They are representing their school or university in a formal manner and should act accordingly. A fan yelling, "Ref, you're horrible!" probably isn't worth bothering with; a cheerleader yelling the same thing is unacceptable.

At more competitive games, cheerleaders may be more vocal, but their job of firing up the crowd should not include berating officials. Notify the game administrator, consider giving one warning, but have them removed for the second offense.

> You're officiating a basketball game. The opening jump ball is a good one, and you're off and running toward the baseline as the lead official. You round the corner near the baseline, eyes focused on the players, to settle into position for the first half-court actions of the game. Suddenly, you're in a collision. Because you're looking where you're supposed to, you don't see the cheerleaders standing on the baseline, and you crash into them. Later, you make a strong block call underneath the basket. You hear someone behind you scream, "That's brutal!" Your head snaps around to find the culprit only to see that there are no fans behind you, just a cheerleader with a doleful look.

Here are some things you can do to avoid any problems with cheerleaders on the court or field:

■ Understand the role of cheerleaders and mascots. Remember that they have worked long hours in preparation for the game, just as the players have. Although cheerleaders are not essential to the game, being dismissive of them only invites conflict.

■ Work with them before the game. Officials are required to be present before the game starts. There is usually ample time to talk to the cheerleaders and their coach or advisor before the game. Cheerleaders tend to position themselves on the baseline at basketball games, which can leave little room on the baseline for the officials. Ask them to move before the game begins so that the game can proceed smoothly.

■ Encourage safety first. If the cheerleaders are hesitant to cooperate, explain to their coach or advisor that their positioning is a safety issue. You're asking them to move to protect them, the players, and the officials from injury. When in doubt, err on the side of safety, as you would in any other potentially dangerous situation.

■ Use the aid of the game administrator. If all else fails, call on the game administrator to help you take care of the situation. Once the administrator understands that you're trying to protect the game's participants—and protect the school from any possible legal liability—the administrator should be cooperative. If problems with the cheerleaders are continual, contact the school's governing body.

Using Warnings and Penalties

You can use informal warnings in situations that are bad enough to warrant attention but not bad enough to penalize. Most of the time, your voice will be effective. Sometimes no amount of preventive officiating resolves a conflict. That's when it's time to use formal warnings or penalties.

Informal Warnings

Many sports have rules that have specific formal warnings for specific infractions that are issued before a penalty. Before you get to that point, you should use informal warnings when possible and appropriate. There are three types of effective informal warnings: the quiet word, the louder word, and the visual warning.

■ *The quiet word.* Use the quiet word when you notice something that could develop into a larger problem, for example, "Captain, number 24 needs to get back to concentrating on playing and letting us officiate. Can you please help us out?" The conversation should include only those directly involved: only the offender or the offender and his or her coach or manager. As you've learned in this chapter, use positive statements and point to a common goal. If you use the quiet word well, you'll likely use it many times throughout the game.

■ *The louder word.* When the quiet word doesn't work, sometimes a louder word does. Be

Even coaches like Lon Kruger, known for being cool and calm (and promoting those traits in their players), can lose patience and insist on being heard. Oblige whenever possible, but don't let your authority be diminished.

firm and strong, but don't ever yell or curse. Consider using the louder word to the offending player in front of other players. "Number 24, I've heard enough," will alert teammates to keep the offender in check.

■ *The visual warning.* When the quiet word and the louder word don't work, use a visual warning. Use a stop gesture—fingers upward and palm extended to the offender—to show all around that you've heard enough and have issued an informal warning. A visual warning, though informal, is considered the last step before issuing a penalty. A smart player or coach will see a stop sign and back off quickly, knowing a penalty is about to be assessed.

Though all three types of informal warnings are great first steps in game management, repeated warnings become ineffective. If you "cry wolf" by continuing to warn without penalizing, eventually the offenders will realize that you're not going to penalize and will ignore your warnings, especially if you repeat the visual warning stage. Ideally, each offender gets one visual warning; the next problem from the same offender should be penalized.

Formal Warnings, Penalties, and Ejections

The rules of some sports indicate formal warnings for specific infractions. Often, the second offense (by the same player or by anyone on the team) results in a penalty. Be sure to study your rule book and understand formal warnings to properly deal with each situation.

One of the most difficult things to sort out as a new official is when to penalize. Each case is different, and officials have different levels of tolerance. Nevertheless, there are a few behaviors that should be penalized automatically every time, though these are rare. For example, a curse word yelled by a player out of personal frustration is often given an automatic penalty at the grade school level. Most of the time, you carefully judge behavior based on such things as game context, severity, and reactions from others.

Here are some behaviors that require an automatic penalty. Remember, in many sports, officials can issue penalties before ejecting an offender. Not all offenses require immediate ejection.

1. *A curse word clearly audible to others.* Occasionally, frustrated players curse to themselves after botching a play. That usually can be handled effectively with a quiet word of caution. However, there are rare times that a player's curse words require a penalty. Generally, if it's loud enough for a distant crowd of people to hear, it's worthy of a penalty, even if not directed toward an official or opponent. For example, if a high school basketball player misses a three-point shot and mutters an expletive out of frustration, a quiet word to the player is sufficient. However, if the player turns toward the crowd and screams an expletive that other players, coaches, and fans clearly hear, a technical foul penalty is appropriate.

2. *Trash talk to an opponent.* Officials play a vital role in encouraging sportsmanship. Part of that role includes penalizing unsportsmanlike behavior. When a player or coach says something derogatory to an opponent, penalize it immediately and without warning.

3. *A coach on the court or field arguing with an official.* In almost all sports, a coach is supposed to be in a specific area. If a coach walks onto the court or field to argue with an official, penalize the coach. Players' and officials' safety can be jeopardized when a coach is on the court or field during play because a dangerous collision could ensue. Also, a coach who chooses to argue on the field or court draws unnecessary attention to the argument and draws other coaches, players, or fans into it. A notable exception is baseball, where tradition dictates a coach may go onto the field to argue with an umpire.

4. *Showing up an official.* If a player or coach is excessively demonstrative while complaining (flailing arms, stomping feet, throwing objects), penalize the offender, especially coaches who throw clipboards or players who throw the game ball. Be sure to watch your partner's back. Sometimes a coach or player waits until the official turns his or her back before visually demonstrating displeasure with overexuberant gestures. If you see such behavior, protect your partner and penalize it, even though the offender wasn't arguing with you.

5. *Anything derogatory that starts with "you."* Do not take personal attacks too lightly. Generally, a coach or player who says, "That's a terrible call!" does not deserve to be penalized. However, if a coach or player says, "You're terrible!" penalize the offender.

6. *Physical contact with an official.* If you are bumped or pushed, eject the offender immediately. There is no second chance.

As you gain experience and learn from others, you'll develop your own limits for what behavior is allowable and what isn't. You don't want a reputation as a "quick trigger," an official who looks for trouble and often penalizes borderline offenses without addressing the problem first. Neither do you want to be labeled as someone who won't "take care of business," an official who lacks the courage to penalize actions that clearly warrant a penalty. You must find the middle ground between the two extremes. Use preventive officiating when appropriate and penalize when necessary.

Here is a simple yet effective guideline: If your concentration is broken by a complaint, it is worth addressing, because your job first and foremost is to take care of the game. After you've spoken to the offender once, if your concentration is broken again by the same offender, penalize.

Some officials seek ways to eject players or coaches. Don't look for trouble; there will be plenty for you to handle without having to look for it. If an ejection is necessary, handle it swiftly and professionally. When ejecting someone, don't get emotional. That's much easier said than done, but think of if it as any other call. If you get wrapped up in emotion, you're more likely to do something that you'll regret later. Keep your cool, and you'll gain respect from peers and participants.

Don't let additional administrative penalties affect your judgment when deciding whether to eject a participant. Many leagues at all levels have adopted automatic suspension rules designed to deter poor behavior. Most of these rules say that when a player or coach is ejected for unsportsmanlike conduct, the offender must sit out the next game. Don't worry that if you eject the offender, he or she will miss another game. The players and coaches are well aware that if they get out of line, they run the risk of missing the next game. If they are not concerned about the additional penalties, you should not concern yourself with them either.

Responding to Violence

In rare instances, game situations turn violent. It's an unfortunate reality that officials must be aware of. In the worst cases, fans brawl with other fans, players go into the stands to confront opposing fans, or a fight breaks out on the court and spills into the stands. When a situation involving brawling fans or players escalates to the point where the game officials and the game administrator can't control it, have the game administrator call the police to restore order. In high-profile sports such as basketball and football at the high school varsity level and above, uniformed police officers often are already assigned to the game site. Know where the police are located so you can find them if you need them.

Assaults against sports officials are drawing unprecedented attention. Many states have passed legislation designed specifically to protect sports officials. Contact the police if you or a partner has been assaulted. File appropriate police reports, and follow through with charges as appropriate. One way to help deter violence against officials is to fight it in the proper way—in the judicial system. You do a disservice to the profession if you're involved in a physical altercation and decide to look the other way to avoid trouble.

Handling Conflict After the Game

Most games end without serious conflict. However, conflict management does not stop when

When to Forfeit

A forfeit (in soccer sometimes called a *termination*) is the most serious call an official can make. You forfeit a game when you've determined that the game can no longer be played under current conditions and that no amount of preventive officiating and penalizing can maintain control of the game. Most sports have specific procedures to follow before ruling a forfeit. Be sure to understand those rules thoroughly to ensure that you handle tough situations appropriately. Ruling a forfeit should always be a last resort. You will likely have few in your career.

© Boothe Davis

Jay Jefferson (left), Pat Clay, and John Queen have their hands full when a fight breaks out during a high school basketball game. Officials must be able to sense volatility rising among players and act accordingly to prevent or contain it.

the game ends. The following sections discuss things you should think about after the game.

Immediately After the Game

Get off the court or field as soon as your officiating duties are over. In most sports, the official's job ends soon after the game ends, but some sports (such as hockey) require officials to watch the teams' postgame handshake.

Hanging around the court or field after a game can invite trouble, even if the game went well in your mind. Remember, sports are competitive, and sometimes competition brings out hostile emotions against officials. Avoid possible postgame conflicts by getting to the locker room or away from participants as soon as the game is over. Always leave with your partners; make sure they are right behind you if you're in the lead to ensure their safety.

Off the Field or Court

Once you're in your locker room, you can begin to unwind mentally. Keep in mind, however, that participants (usually coaches) are sometimes so unhappy that they'll want to enter your locker room to confront you. Ideally, only officials and possibly a game administrator should be allowed into the officials' locker room. Don't let anyone else in to discuss your officiating or the game, not even the home coach if possible.

Because of space limitations, many times your locker room is the home coach's office. In this case, before the game, ask the game administrator to have the coach wait until after the officials have left the premises to get into his or her office after the game. If a coach does enter your locker room, as frequently happens in shared space at grade school or high school levels, avoid conversation. Be polite if any response is necessary. If

What to Do if You're Attacked

If you are physically attacked in connection with your officiating, you should know what to do and what not to do. In an interview with *Referee* magazine, Mel Narol, an attorney who is an authority on legal issues involving officials, gave advice on the proper procedures for handling the legal aspects of an assault:

1. Don't strike back to attack the player, coach, or fan who assaulted you. If your attacker is injured by your retaliation, you could be subject to criminal liability or a reduction of a potential monetary award. By fighting back physically, you may be placing yourself in a no-win situation.

2. As soon as possible, obtain the names, addresses, and phone numbers of witnesses. The information they supply may be critical to you and your attorney.

3. Immediately write down the complete history of what occurred and how you were injured. Be sure to include the names, addresses, and phone numbers of everyone who was present, including your attackers if known, coaches and managers, other officials, and game attendants.

4. Determine whether a videotape of the game and incident were made; if so, obtain a copy of that tape. Visual evidence can be of great value to you and your attorney.

5. Don't discuss the incident with anyone; simply gather information. Often what you say is misunderstood or misinterpreted, which may return to haunt you during litigation.

6. Obtain competent legal counsel. Discuss whether you have a civil or criminal complaint to make against your attackers. If you are assaulted during or after a game that you've worked, you have the right to pursue both civil and criminal actions. Those options should be discussed with legal counsel.

the coach begins an inappropriate discussion about the game or your officiating, ask the coach to leave the locker room until the officials have left. If the problem escalates, contact the governing body (league administrator, assignor, or state association, for example) to report the incident.

When you leave your locker room and head for the parking lot, be sure to do so with your partners or an escort if possible. In rare cases, upset people linger in the parking lot after a game to confront officials. Having other people around will help control the situation, and they can serve as witnesses in the event of a confrontation. In cold weather, make sure all your partners' cars start properly before leaving the premises.

Reporting Conflicts

Writing reports is becoming commonplace in officiating today. More frequently than in the past, officials are required to submit misconduct reports to schools, league offices, or governing bodies, such as a state high school association. Some organizations require officials to submit a game report after every game, even if there was no misconduct to report.

Why so many reports? The reports are usually used to protect officials, school personnel, and other responsible entities from legal liability. Thirty years ago, it was rare for a game incident to end up in court. Today, it's more commonplace. If you're involved in a court case, you probably will be asked to reconstruct the incident—possibly months or years after it happened. That's a difficult, if not impossible, task without a report written just after the incident.

If you've had an unsportsmanlike incident during a game, call the league administrator or assignor first, before sending a written report. Most administrators want to hear about incidents from officials first—before an angry coach calls—so that they can deal with the angry coach appropriately. Don't let your assignor be surprised by a coach's phone call if you have time to give the assignor advance warning about the situation.

Misconduct Reports

Send misconduct reports or incident reports to the proper authorities, even if reports are not re-

Post-Game Evaluation

After any game involving an ejection or other unsportsmanlike conduct, ask yourself these important questions:

1. Did I do anything to lead to the ejection?

2. Did I challenge the player or coach?

3. Did I lose self-control?

4. Did my body language show that I was the aggressor?

5. Did I let the coach or player have a chance to get his or her emotions in check?

6. Will I do anything differently the next time something similar occurs?

Take a hard look at yourself to see what you could have done better. Ask your partners for their views, or review the incident with respected veterans to gain further insight. Some bad situations can't be prevented, but many can.

After your self-analysis, your next challenge is preparing mentally for your next game. You must learn from the incident, but you also must clear your head to officiate the next game. The biggest challenge is the next time that you must work with the offender. You'll find that often the incident has been forgotten by the offender; you need to forget it too. Even if the offender's bad feelings have festered, you must remain professional and implement your conflict management plan. It's unfair to the participants to allow your bad feelings to carry over from one game to the next.

quired. Report any ejection, flagrant foul, unsportsmanlike conduct, or unruly fan behavior. Reporting such incidents accomplishes two important things: You write down the facts immediately after the incident, and you cover your bases by reporting it.

Some officials look at writing reports as a laborious chore, but officials risk forgetting key information if they're required to reconstruct an incident much later and a report was not written. Equally important, officials who do not write reports do an injustice to other officials. If an official doesn't identify an offender in a misconduct report, the proper authorities and other officials may not know about the problem and cannot track patterns of poor behavior.

Game Reports

Game reports are different from misconduct reports but are equally important. In some conferences or leagues, game reports are required from officials after every contest. Game reports are not always negative. Game reports identify patterns of problem behavior and player injuries but also note positive experiences and good sportsmanship.

Writing Your Report

There's no need to report every cross word you have with a coach or player, but when in doubt, file an incident report. These are some details that should appear in each report:

1. Date and time of the incident

2. The game site

3. The names of all the officials involved, the names of the teams, and, if possible, the names of the head coaches

4. Weather conditions (if played outdoors)

5. Field or court conditions

6. Light conditions, especially if the light was a factor (for example, a softball game finishing at dusk)

7. Game situation at time of incident (for example, the inning or time left in the period)

8. Detailed description of incident or injury, including whether and by whom medical attention was given

9. If possible, names or numbers of players involved

10. Additional notes or diagrams if necessary and events that led to the incident if relevant

The tone you set in your report is very important. It reflects on your credibility. Stick to the facts. Don't exaggerate, make unprovable statements, or arrive at unfounded conclusions, for example, "He approached the player with anger in his eyes and punched him." Avoid vague or subjective terms such as, "The coach lost total control of himself." Relate only what you observe. Don't bring up hearsay or past experiences unless they're directly related to the incident at hand. Don't speculate, as in "The players' actions are a direct result of the coach's lack of control." Report the events in the order they took place,

but don't add unprovable opinions about cause and effect.

Avoid recommending a course of action, such as, "The coach should be suspended for his actions." The official's job is to relate the facts, not pass judgment. Let the appropriate authorities handle the punishment. Also, don't threaten: "If someone doesn't stop this team from acting as they do, I'm not going to work any more of their games. I'll spread the word at my local officials' association, and soon no one will work for this team." Threats diminish your credibility. Keep in mind that what you're reporting is likely not typical behavior.

Jot down pertinent information as soon as possible after the game while the incident is fresh in your mind; the longer you wait, the more you'll forget. Compare thoughts with your partners. Bring a note pad and pen to each game so you're ready if you need them. Tape recorders are also handy tools.

After you've written the report, let it sit for a while and think about something else. Consider having another respected official read it to provide input. Reread the report as if you were the person receiving it. Does it clearly convey what happened? Is it credible? Does it have the proper tone? If so, you're ready to send it. If not, fix

Sample Journal Entry

Time	Action	Comments
Third inning	Called time when pitcher started delivery	The coach was correct in objecting I may have been too late
Fifth inning	Didn't go out far enough on line drive	It may have been trapped I should have ignored coach's complaint instead of defending my action
Seventh inning	Catcher spoke sarcastically to batter	I should have warned him and reminded the coach between innings to speak to his catcher

what's necessary. Keep a copy of your report. You may be asked later to clarify your statements or reconstruct the incident. Also, follow up with the governing body. You have a right to know what action was taken following an incident.

Postseason Management

During the course of the season, keep a journal. Write down strange plays, your feelings about your performance, notes about your partner, things you did well, and things you can improve. A journal is a great way to look back during and after the season to see whether you have patterns of behavior that need adjusting. If the same problems keep appearing in your journal, you know those things need to be addressed. Reviewing the journal is also a great way to start thinking about officiating and your conflict management plan before your next season. See the sample entry on page 83 for an example.

Summary

Knowing the rules and mechanics isn't enough; it's how you handle people that makes a difference. The best officials are good not only at calling fouls, violations, safes, and outs. They can defuse hostility and keep players and coaches in games, but they have the courage to penalize when necessary. Plan how you will handle conflict. It helps to understand why people treat officials as they do. Implement your plan, and use preventive officiating whenever possible. Deal with people dispassionately and professionally at all times. Learn from each situation.

Conflict management is an important psychological skill for officiating. To become a complete official, you need to prepare both psychologically and physically. The next part of the book discusses physical fitness and why it is important for officials.

Part III
....

Personal Fitness for Officials

7

Fitness Principles for Officials

Jon Poole and Kathleen Poole

In this chapter you'll learn

- the four components of health-related physical fitness,
- the importance of staying injury free,
- how healthy nutrition can improve your officiating performance, and
- how physical fitness and health are affected by aging.

Recommendations for improving health-related physical fitness come from organizations such as the Department of Health and Human Services' Surgeon General's Report, the American College of Sports Medicine, the Centers for Disease Control and Prevention, the President's Council on Physical Fitness and Sports, and the Cooper Institute for Aerobics Research.

Health-Related Physical Fitness

The 1996 Surgeon General's Report from the Department of Health and Human Services positively linked daily physical activity with increased overall health. Premature death and illness are associated with sedentary lifestyles. It is unrealistic to abuse your body with poor eating and sedentary living during the off-season, then expect it to respond to a month or two of vigorous conditioning and dieting as the preseason nears. Instead, walking and other exercise activities need to become daily habits, along with healthy eating and a commitment to specific exercises that improve flexibility and muscle fitness.

A combination of health-related components make up what many people think of as physical fitness. These are the four components of health-related physical fitness:

1. *Cardiorespiratory fitness*, the ability of the body to perform prolonged large-muscle-mass activities at moderate to vigorous intensity,

2. *Muscular fitness*, the ability of the muscles to perform forcefully (muscular strength) and repeatedly over time (muscular endurance),

3. *Flexibility*, the ability of the joints to move through a full range of motion, and

4. *Body composition*, the percentage of lean body mass (bone, water, muscle, connective tissue, organ tissues, and teeth) to total body fat.

When preparing to become physically fit, you should consider several principles of physical training, including specificity, progressive overload, and reversibility. Specificity simply means that your workouts must use the specific fitness component that you wish to improve. Weight training is wonderful for muscular fitness, for example, but not the best choice for cardiorespiratory fitness. Similarly, running is wonderful for cardiorespiratory fitness, but not the best for flexibility.

Progressive overload means that to continually improve your fitness, you must progressively increase the exercise load as your body adapts to each of the demands placed upon it. The amount of overload is critical. Too much exercise can result in injury, and too little results in limited fitness gains. To determine the proper amount of exercise, consider the FIT principles: frequency, intensity, and time. Frequency refers to how often during the week you exercise, intensity refers to how hard you exercise, and time refers to how long you exercise at any given session.

Reversibility is the opposite of the adaptation your body makes as you increase physical stress to improve fitness. That is, as you become more sedentary, your body quickly loses, or reverses, your previous fitness gains. More than 50 percent of the improvement from a fitness program can be lost within eight weeks of ending a program. This is why it is so important that physical activity becomes a lifestyle habit and not just something you do to get ready for a season of officiating. Choose physical activities that you find enjoyable and that suit your lifestyle, geographic area, and financial budget.

Cardiorespiratory Fitness

The ability to maintain prolonged physical activity means that your body is more efficient in performing daily tasks and better able to handle physical challenges. The benefits of aerobic exercise (i.e., large-muscle activities performed for a prolonged period, such as 15 to 20 minutes or more) include improved blood circulation, decreased blood pressure, improved metabolism, decreased body fat, better adaptation to stress and anxiety, and better performance in sport-related activities (including officiating).

The tragic on-field death of 328-pound umpire John McSherry from a massive heart attack on opening day of the 1996 major league baseball season clearly signaled the need for every official, indeed every adult, to consider the costs of poor cardiorespiratory fitness. Poor cardiorespiratory fitness is especially harmful for officials who work in extremely hot and humid conditions or those who officiate sports that require a great deal of running, such as soccer or basketball. In addition, much as you might expect more errors (especially mental errors) from players who experience fatigue in the latter stages of a contest, you can also expect officials more likely to make mistakes due to fatigue. Thus, cardiorespiratory fitness is critical for officiating success.

Improving and Maintaining Cardiorespiratory Fitness

Recent recommendations suggest that all adults should undertake at least 30 minutes of moderate-intensity physical activity every day to improve their overall health. Suggested daily activities include moderate-paced walking, yard work, and less reliance on modern conveniences such as elevators and escalators. To truly enhance cardiorespiratory fitness, however, a greater commitment must be made to more-intense physical activities, such as swimming, running, cycling, cross-country skiing, and walking vigorously. A basic guideline is that aerobic exercise should be performed three to five days per week to improve overall physical fitness.

Muscular Fitness

The ability to exert forceful and prolonged muscular contractions means that your body will not tire easily and will be better able to handle the routine tasks and physical challenges of officiating. The benefits of muscular fitness exercises include improved oxygen delivery to working muscles, improved metabolism, decreased body fat, lower risk of injury, and better performance in sport-related activities, including officiating.

Improving and Maintaining Muscular Fitness

Recent recommendations suggest that adults should perform muscular fitness exercises two to three times per week to improve their overall health. Suggested exercises include push-ups, pull-ups, horizontal-bar dips, single-leg lunges, and abdominal crunches. To truly enhance muscular fitness, a commitment must be made to a greater variety of exercises that include reliance on strength-training equipment, such as barbells and dumbbells, exercise tubes, or home gyms. Specific training guidelines to improve muscle fitness are discussed in the next chapter.

Flexibility

Flexibility is probably most important for overall joint health and prevention of injuries. Certain sport activities, such as gymnastics and diving, depend highly on flexibility for improved performance. For officiating, flexibility is probably less important for performance than for injury prevention. Additional benefits of flexibility include the stress-reducing qualities of stretching exercises and the reduction of postexercise muscle soreness when light stretching is included in an overall fitness plan.

Improving and Maintaining Flexibility

Recent recommendations suggest that adults should perform at least 15 minutes of flexibility exercises in conjunction with their three- to five-times-weekly cardiorespiratory and muscle-fitness workouts. Traditionally, stretching exercises were performed before a warm-up or were considered the actual warm-up. Recent evidence supports first warming the body up with walking, jogging, easy rope jumping, or a similar activity to prepare for being physically active. Only after a warm-up should you attempt stretching exercises. Stretching cold muscles before a warm-up can lead to a greater rather than a reduced chance

of injury. Most officials depend primarily on their lower body to run up and down a court or field, so pre- and postgame stretching routines should specifically address your legs. Specific flexibility exercises are presented in the next chapter.

Body Composition

Body composition is important to your ability to move efficiently and feel good about yourself. Unfortunately, our society has been led to believe that body weight (and not body composition) is related to health and success. Height and weight charts are, at best, arbitrary estimates of what males and females should weigh according to height and estimated frame size. Body weight does not account for the amount of lean body mass, and highly muscled individuals are thus unfairly classified as overweight, because muscle weighs more than fat. Conversely, an unfit individual may be classified as having a healthy body weight when in reality his or her body composition may be overfat. Another consideration, perhaps unfair, is the negative public perception of officials who are overweight. Officials are part of the spectacle that is sport (especially at a collegiate or professional level), and an official who appears overweight is not seen in the same positive light as an official who appears fit and trim.

Improving and Maintaining a Healthy Body Composition

Recent recommendations suggest that females should strive to keep their body fat under 32 percent; a more desirable range is between 15 and 25 percent. Males should strive to keep their body fat under 25 percent; a more desirable range for males is between 10 and 20 percent. Highly fit individuals may have under 10 percent body fat, but it is considered a threat to health and well-being if body fat drops below 5 percent for men or 8 percent for women. Body composition is best altered through a combination of healthy eating and a physically active lifestyle. A deficit of just 500 calories a day, which is roughly equivalent to many fast-food sandwiches or running for 30 to 45 minutes, results in a weight loss of three to five pounds per month. This healthy and safe method of eating a little more appropriately and exercising a little more every day helps to make

Body composition not only affects you physically. It affects people's perceptions of you as an official.

exercises that mirror the particular officiating moves found in your sport (e.g., short, quick, sliding movements for basketball officials). If you are not fit, it is unreasonable to expect your body to perform at the level needed to officiate and still stay injury free. Poor fitness can lead to both acute and chronic injuries. Even if an official avoids acute injuries, the repetitive motions of officiating can still lead to a chronic injury.

Additional attention should be paid to eyewear and footwear. Eyewear should be unbreakable and include straps to hold it in place. Good footwear should provide proper support, cushioning, and traction. The use of orthotics in shoes to maintain correct foot and lower-extremity alignment during activity may be necessary. Heel lifts should be considered to prevent Achilles tendon and calf injuries. As shoes become worn, they lose cushioning properties and offer poor support and traction. Worn shoes can lead to chronic injuries, such as tendinitis and stress fractures, as well as acute injuries caused by loss of support and poor traction.

Pay close attention to signals from your body. Aches and pains before, during, and after exercise, especially those involving tendons and joints, should be evaluated to determine their cause and correctability before serious injury occurs. Common injuries for officials and treatments for their care are discussed in the next chapter.

physical fitness a habit, which is preferable to an unreasonable diet or exercise plan that does not fit into your normal lifestyle.

Staying Injury Free

Injury prevention is important to all officials but becomes even more important as an official ages. As we age, even minor mishaps can result in severe injuries. A seemingly minor injury can bring an officiating career to an end.

Injuries can be caused by muscle imbalance, poor muscle fitness, poor flexibility, poor cardiorespiratory fitness, improper equipment, or inadequate rehabilitation following a prior injury. The most important way to stay injury free is to maintain a healthy lifestyle that includes a regular fitness program. You should perform specific

Healthy Eating

Nutrition is an essential component of wellness. The foods that we eat affect our energy levels, thereby influencing physical performance, well-being, and overall health. Our diet can also place us at greater risk for major chronic diseases such as cancer, cardiovascular disease, and diabetes, as well as a host of other health problems. The good news is that a well-planned diet combined with regular physical activity can help prevent these diseases and even reverse some of them.

Six Classes of Essential Nutrients

Our bodies require many substances to function properly. We require nutrients, which are substances that the body needs for the maintenance of health, growth, and repair of tissues. Nutrients can be classified into six categories:

■ carbohydrates,

■ fats,

■ proteins,

■ vitamins,

■ minerals, and

■ water.

Three of these classes of nutrients actually provide energy: carbohydrates, proteins, and fats. Fats supply the most energy—nine calories per gram—whereas carbohydrate and protein supply four calories per gram. High-fat diets (more than 30 percent of calories from fat) are not recommended because they place us at greater risk for a variety of diseases, such as cancer, heart disease, stroke, and diabetes. Because high-fat diets supply more calories, they are associated with an increased prevalence of obesity. Health experts recommend that fat intake be less than 30 percent of total daily calories, with no more than 10 percent of these fat calories from saturated fat. Saturated fats come predominantly from animal sources and are usually solid at room temperature. Plant sources of saturated fat include palm oil, palm kernel oil, coconut oil, and cocoa butter. A diet high in saturated fats is associated with an increased risk of cardiovascular disease.

Proteins are essential components of cell membranes, muscle, bone, blood, enzymes, and some hormones. A well-balanced diet should get about 10 to 15 percent of its calories from protein. Many Americans consume much more than that every day. Excess protein is synthesized into fat to be used as energy or stored in the body. Extra protein is usually not harmful for most Americans; however, many foods high in protein are also high in fat. The protein requirement for adults is generally met by consuming 0.8 grams of protein per kilogram of body weight. The American Dietetic Association (ADA) recommends that a person who is training intensely consume 1.0 to 1.5 grams of protein per kilogram of body weight. Additional protein should be obtained through food choices, not through supplements. According to the ADA, "Excessive protein intake, either through consumption of high protein foods or protein/amino acid supplements, is unnecessary, does not contribute to athletic performance or increased muscle mass, and actually may be detrimental to health and athletic performance."

The primary function of carbohydrates is to supply energy to the cells of the body. During high-intensity exercise, our muscles get most of their energy from carbohydrates. Fruits, vegetables, and grains are excellent sources of carbohydrates. A well-balanced diet should get about 55 to 60 percent of calories from carbohydrates. No more than 10 percent of carbohydrate calories should come from simple sugars such as those found in candy and sodas. Complex carbohydrates are more nutritionally dense than simple carbohydrates. That is, complex carbohydrates contain more essential nutrients. Another benefit of eating more complex carbohydrates is that

Are Sports Drinks Better Than Water to Rehydrate and Replenish Electrolytes?

In general, water is the fluid-replacement drink of choice. According to the ACSM, "There is little need to replace electrolytes lost during most brief exercise sessions since these small decrements are typically replenished when the next meal is eaten." Unless the exercise bout lasts more than 60 minutes, there is little need to supplement carbohydrates. For continuous, vigorous activity lasting 60 minutes or more, the American College of Sports Medicine recommends consuming a solution containing 4 to 8 percent carbohydrates (glucose, sucrose, or starch). The solution should be ingested in small to moderate quantities (6 to 12 ounces) every 15 to 20 minutes during vigorous activity.

Insights on Vision

"Are ya blind ump?" "Where were you looking?" "How couldn't you've seen that when everybody else in the world saw it?" Vision care is an important part of your health as an official. Dr. Bradley Rounds, Behavioral optometrist, has worked with professional golfers, trap shooters, and members of the US Olympic ski team. He has this to say about officiating and vision:

Vision can be a relative thing. Depending on which side of the ball you're on, which side the field you're on or who your relatives are, people will see things differently. The problem is, *you* have to see it correctly. You don't have the benefit of "reverse angle" or "ultra slow motion"; you must make the split-second decision and get it right. The only tools you have are your intellect, your experience, and your vision.

Twenty/twenty is not perfect vision. Your "eyesight" is pretty much a given thing, be it 20/20 or 20/400. The good thing is, it can be corrected with spectacles, contact lenses or even with surgery. But, eyesight is just one part of vision. *Vision* incorporates eyesight, focusing, eye-movement, spatial orientation, and visual perception. Focusing and eye-movements require fine motor movements. Like occupational therapy and physical therapy, vision therapy works to re-teach or enhance these fine motor skills for the utmost precision and efficiency. All components of vision, with the exception of eyesight, are learned through trial and error throughout life. Since vision is learned, it can be "relearned", or enhanced through therapy. Visual perception and spatial orientation can be enhanced by improving these visual skills and through use of special training aides. Many professional and collegiate athletes have improved their performance with vision therapy (orthoptics). As an official, your vision is just as important as an athlete's, and therefore must be treated with the same seriousness.

To have your vision tested, see an optometrist specializing in sports vision. These doctors are trained to see the patient as a whole being, not just two eyeballs. They will check ocular health, prescribe corrective devices or design a plan for vision enhancement training. The American Optometric Association recommends a yearly vision and ocular health examination. It is also recommended that proper eye protection be worn at all time when engaged in sports or sport officiating. Contact the AOA's Sports Vision Section or the International Academy of Sports Vision to find an optometrist near you. Ask your optometrist to prescribe exercises specific to your vision needs as an official.

they are typically excellent sources of dietary fiber. Fiber helps prevent cancers of the digestive system, hemorrhoids, constipation, and diverticular diseases because it helps food move more easily and quickly through the digestive system. The recommended daily intake of fiber is 20 to 35 grams. Sources include whole grains, vegetables, fruits, and legumes.

Water plays an essential role in the normal functioning of the body. The human body is about 60 percent water. Water is necessary to regulate temperature and transport substances throughout the body. It is recommended that individuals should consume about two liters, or eight cups, of water per day. This need is higher for those who exercise intensely.

Proper hydration is particularly important for officials. Sweating is the body's primary method for heat dissipation during exercise. The amount of sweat lost during exercise depends on the heat and humidity, type and intensity of activity, and other factors that vary from individual to individual. Dehydration decreases the body's ability to sweat and can result in impaired performance by reducing coordination, strength, and endurance. Further, dehydration increases a person's risk of heat stroke, heat exhaustion, and heat cramps. The American College of Sports Medicine (ACSM) and the ADA recommend drinking two cups of water two hours before exercising and two more cups within 15 minutes of beginning an endurance exercise session. During exercise, you should consume about 150 milliliters (about six ounces) of water every 15 minutes, particularly in hot and humid weather. Water should be cold (45 to 55 degrees Fahrenheit).

The Food Guide Pyramid

The Food Guide Pyramid was developed by the United States Department of Agriculture (USDA) in 1992. The pyramid is routinely found on cereal boxes, cookie and cracker boxes, and bread bags. Seven core dietary guidelines (healthy eating choices) recommended by the USDA and others include:

1. *Choose a variety of foods.* Select from the six food groups shown on the pyramid, and eat the appropriate number of servings for each group. Check the nutritional information in your food to ensure that you are eating from the right group and are getting the appropriate serving sizes.

2. *Choose to balance food intake with moderate, daily physical activity.* This will help you maintain

The Food Guide Pyramid
A Guide to Daily Food Choices

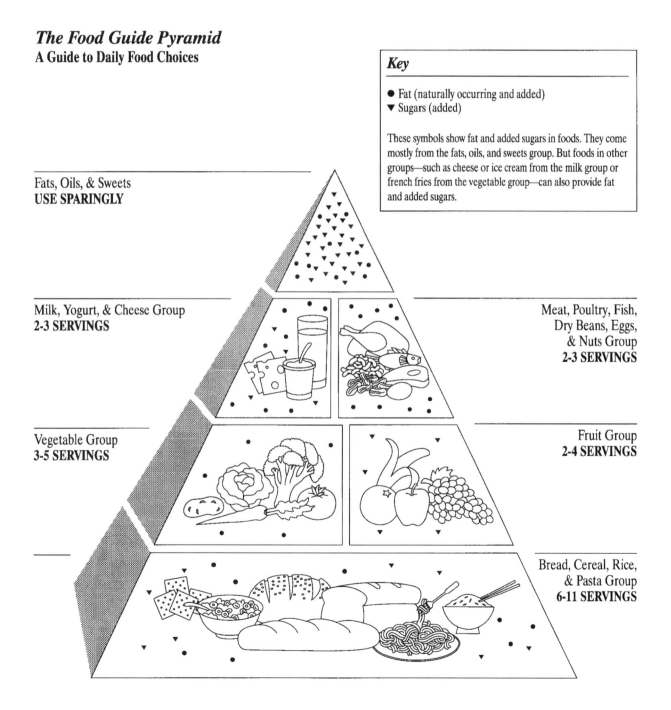

Key

● Fat (naturally occurring and added)
▼ Sugars (added)

These symbols show fat and added sugars in foods. They come mostly from the fats, oils, and sweets group. But foods in other groups—such as cheese or ice cream from the milk group or french fries from the vegetable group—can also provide fat and added sugars.

Fats, Oils, & Sweets
USE SPARINGLY

Milk, Yogurt, & Cheese Group
2-3 SERVINGS

Meat, Poultry, Fish, Dry Beans, Eggs, & Nuts Group
2-3 SERVINGS

Vegetable Group
3-5 SERVINGS

Fruit Group
2-4 SERVINGS

Bread, Cereal, Rice, & Pasta Group
6-11 SERVINGS

proper body weight. Increased weight in adulthood results in increased risk of diabetes, heart disease, cancer, and other diseases. As you age, you need to increase the duration of physical activity to keep up with a steadily decreasing metabolism.

3. *Choose a majority of foods from the bottom of the pyramid.* Grain products, fruits, and vegetables tend to be low in fat and high in complex carbohydrates, dietary fiber, vitamins, and minerals.

4. *Choose foods low in fat, saturated fat, and cholesterol.* Fat intake should not exceed 30 percent of your total calories per day, and saturated fat should not exceed one third of your total daily fat intake. Dietary cholesterol should be limited to 300 milligrams per day.

5. *Choose foods high in sugar sparingly.* Foods high in sugar often do not provide much in the way of nutritional value and also promote tooth decay. High-sugar beverages like colas and fruit punch should be consumed sparingly.

6. *Choose foods high in salt and sodium sparingly.* Many Americans consume more than 10 times the needed sodium per day. Only very small

Mark Gilchrist (left) and Fred Gallagher appreciate a trainer's thoughtfulness. On hot days be sure to drink lots of fluids before the game as well.

amounts of salt should be added to food at the table. Try adding pepper or other spices to enhance the flavor of you food.

7. *Choose alcoholic beverages in moderation.* While some evidence has linked moderate alcohol consumption with lower risk for heart disease in some people, higher levels of consumption are associated with higher mortality rates and disease prevalence.

Staying Physically Fit as You Age

Remaining physically active actually delays the onset of the aging process. Equally important, the benefits of physical activity—such as fewer illnesses, fewer posture problems, greater joint mobility, and less chance of osteoporosis—can help an older person feel younger.

As you move through life, you can expect some loss in your functional capability as an official, for example, your ability to move as quickly as when you were younger, your ability to remain injury free, and your ability to maintain peak physical conditioning. All four components of health-related physical fitness are negatively affected by the aging process. Joints begin to stiffen and lose mobility, muscles lose strength, and the metabolism slows down, making it harder to control weight. Luckily for you, however, this loss in functional capability is not completely age dependent, but is often lifestyle dependent. Remaining active and continuing to eat healthy foods will delay most of the negative effects of aging. Further, with experience on the field or court, you will learn how to move more efficiently to position yourself to make an appropriate call.

It is no wonder that many veteran officials continue to dominate play-off and championship games, not because they are in better physical condition than their younger colleagues, but rather because they have continued to learn to be better officials. However, those veteran officials who maintain a high level of physical fitness assure themselves of long and, with luck, injury-free careers. Following the personal fitness plan you develop in the next chapter will go a long way in helping you to maintain the physically active and healthy lifestyle needed to succeed in officiating and to ensure a high-quality life.

Summary

This chapter discussed the key benefits of improving and maintaining your health-related physical fitness, thereby improving your officiating and helping you to enjoy a long career. The key focus was making physical activity and healthy eating regular habits. The next chapter will help you design a personal fitness plan that will help you prevent injuries and improve all four components of physical fitness.

Your Personal Fitness Plan

Jon Poole, Kathleen Poole, and Doug Toole

In this chapter you'll learn

■ how to design your own personal fitness plan,

■ the four components of your physical workout,

■ stretching exercises to improve your flexibility,

■ 8 strength exercises to improve your muscular fitness, and

■ treatments for injuries common among sports officials.

Designing your personal fitness plan involves three basic steps: (1) self-assessment, (2) goal setting, and (3) selection of physical activities. Self-assessment helps you determine your readiness to begin an exercise program and your current fitness levels. Next, you decide what you hope to accomplish with your fitness plan and the components of fitness that you would like to improve. Finally, you select the physical activities that will best help you meet your goals.

Self-Assessment

To ensure that your fitness program is appropriate for you, it is wise to assess your current level of fitness. The following sections provide self-assessment tools that you can use to determine your readiness to begin an exercise program and your fitness levels in each of the four areas of health-related fitness. (The four components of physical fitness—cardiorespiratory fitness, muscular fitness, flexibility, and body composition—are described in chapter 7.)

General Readiness Self-Assessment

To determine whether exercise is safe for you, see if you have any of the conditions listed below (Are You Ready for Physical Activity?). If you do have any of the conditions on the list or are over 65 and are not accustomed to vigorous exercise, postpone vigorous exercise or exercise testing until after you have consulted your doctor.

Cardiorespiratory Fitness Self-Assessment

There are many cardiorespiratory fitness tests available today (you may remember some from your days in physical education class). The simplest is probably the one-mile walk test. This test requires you to walk a measured mile on a track or a relatively flat course. You also need a stopwatch and a heart rate monitor, if possible, and you must know your body weight.

Follow these steps to perform the one-mile walk test.

1. Warm up briefly before taking this test with some easy walking or light jogging, followed by a few stretching exercises specifically for the lower body.

2. Walk the one-mile distance as quickly as possible, at a pace that is brisk yet comfortable and raises your heart rate over 120 beats per minute.

3. As soon as you complete the distance, note

your time, and take your pulse for 15 seconds. Continue to cool down with slow walking for several minutes.

4. Walking time: _____ minutes _____ seconds

5. Heart rate: _____ beats per minute (multiply 15-second pulse count by 4)

6. Convert your time from minutes and seconds to minutes as a decimal figure. For example, a time of 13 minutes and 26 seconds is 13 + (26/60), or 13.43 minutes.

7. Determine your maximal oxygen consumption ($\dot{V}O_2$max) by inserting your age (A), sex (S; male = 1, female = 0), weight in pounds (W), walking time (T), and exercise heart rate (H) into the following equation.

$$\dot{V}O_2 \text{ max} = 132.853 - (0.0769 \times W) - (0.3877 \times A) + (6.315 \times S) - (3.2649 \times T) - (0.1565 \times H)$$

Enter your cardiorespiratory fitness score on the form provided at the end of this chapter on (p. 114).

Muscular Fitness Self-Assessment

True assessment of muscular strength would require determining a single-repetition maximum (1RM) for exercises such as the bench press and

Are You Ready for Physical Activity?

We recommend that you postpone vigorous exercise or exercise testing if you have or have had one or more of the following:

- High blood pressure
- Chest pains
- Heart trouble
- Bone or joint problems
- Dizzy spells
- Arthritis
- Weight problems (overweight or underweight)

YMCA Norms for Resting Heart Rate (beats/min)

Age (yr)	18–25		26–35		36–45		46–55		56–65		>65	
Gender	M	F	M	F	M	F	M	F	M	F	M	F
Excellent	49–55	54–60	49–54	54–59	50–56	54–59	50–57	54–60	51–56	54–59	50–55	54–59
Good	57–61	61–65	57–61	60–64	60–62	62–64	59–63	61–65	59–61	61–64	58–61	60–64
Above average	63–65	66–69	62–65	66–68	64–66	66–69	64–67	66–69	64–67	67–69	62–65	66–68
Average	67–69	70–73	66–70	69–71	68–70	70–72	68–71	70–73	68–71	71–73	66–69	70–72
Below average	71–73	74–78	72–74	72–76	73–76	74–78	73–76	74–77	72–75	75–77	70–73	73–76
Poor	76–81	80–84	77–81	78–82	77–82	79–82	79–83	78–84	76–81	79–81	75–79	79–84
Very poor	84–95	86–100	84–94	84–94	86–96	84–92	85–97	85–96	84–94	85–96	83–98	88–96

Source: Adapted from: YMCA. *Y's Way to Fitness.* 3rd edition. Reprinted with permission from the YMCA of the USA.

squat. Since there is great potential for injury when attempting a 1RM, we do not advocate this assessment. Instead, we focus on muscular endurance, which can be assessed safely without any special equipment.

Norms in the above chart were established with men completing standard push-ups and women completing modified push-ups (supporting yourself on your knees).

The Push-Up Test

Follow these steps to complete the push-up test.

1. On a carpeted floor or exercise mat, perform the maximum number of push-ups that you possibly can.

2. From the starting position, with hands roughly shoulder-width apart and fingers

Male Norms for the Push-Up Test (number completed)

Rating	Age (years)				
	20–29	30–39	40–49	50–59	60–69
Above average	29–35	22–29	17–21	13–20	11–17
Average	22–28	17–21	13–16	10–12	8–10
Below average	17–21	12–16	10–12	7–9	5–7
Low	≤ 16	≤ 11	≤ 9	≤ 6	≤ 4

From the *ACSM Fitness Book,* 2nd edition, Human Kinetics, 1998, p. 34. Used by permission.

Female Norms for the Push-Up Test (number completed)

Rating	Age (years)				
	20–29	30–39	40–49	50–59	60–69
Above average	21–29	20–26	15–23	11–20	12–16
Average	15–20	13–19	11–14	7–10	5–11
Below average	10–14	8–12	5–10	2–6	1–4
Low	≤ 9	≤ 7	≤ 9	≤ 1	≤ 1

From the *ACSM Fitness Book,* 2nd edition, Human Kinetics, 1998, p. 34. Used by permission.

pointing forward, lower your chest to the floor, keeping your back straight. Then return to the starting position.

3. Perform as many push-ups as possible without stopping.

4. Record your maximum number of push-ups: _____

Enter your muscular fitness score on the form provided at the end of this chapter (p. 114).

Flexibility Self-Assessment

Your flexibility varies across different joints, but the generally accepted test for flexibility is the sit-and-reach test of lower-back and hamstring flexibility. This test is best done with the assistance of a partner.

The Sit-and-Reach Test

Follow these steps to complete the sit-and-reach test.

1. Remove your shoes, and sit on a carpeted floor or exercise mat with your legs stretched in front of you about 10 to 12 inches apart. Position a yardstick between your feet with the zero mark toward you so that the soles of your feet are even with the 15-inch mark.

2. From the starting position, with your knees straight, hands one on top of the other, and

palms down, reach forward as far as possible, and hold this maximum reach for one to two seconds. Keep your knees locked throughout the test.

3. Record the farthest point reached with the fingertips of both your hands. Number of inches: _____

Enter your flexibility fitness score on the form provided at the end of this chapter (p. 114).

Body Composition Self-Assessment

The most common and accurate measures of body composition in health and fitness clubs include underwater weighing and bioelectrical impedance. Another way to assess body composition is to measure skinfold thickness with a caliper. All these methods, though fairly accurate, are also extremely difficult for self-assessment. We advocate measuring body mass index (BMI) and waist-to-hip ratio for self-assessment, because they do not require sophisticated equipment.

Body Mass Index

Body mass index (BMI) is a measurement that indicates your weight-related level of risk for developing heart disease, high blood pressure, or diabetes.

1. Measure your height in inches and weight in pounds, and record those results.

   Height: _____ Weight: _____

Modified Sit-and-Reach

Score at age:	20–29	30–39	40–49	50–59	60+
Men					
High	19	18	17	16	15
Average	13–18	12–17	11–16	10–15	9–14
Below average	10–12	9–11	8–10	7–9	6–8
Low	≤ 9	≤ 8	≤ 7	≤ 6	≤ 5
Women					
High	22	21	20	19	18
Average	16–21	15–20	14–19	13–18	12–17
Below average	13–15	12–14	11–13	10–12	9–11
Low	≤ 12	≤ 11	≤ 10	≤ 9	≤ 8

From the *ACSM Fitness Book,* 2nd edition, Human Kinetics, 1998, p. 37. Used by permission.

2. Multiply your weight in pounds (W) by 705. Divide the result by your height in inches (H); then divide that result by your height in inches (H) again.

BMI = W × 705/H/H

A BMI of 25 or less is considered very low to low risk. A BMI of 25 to 30 is low to moderate risk. A BMI of 30 or more is moderate to very high risk. Enter your BMI on the form provided at the end of this chapter (p. 114).

Waist-to-Hip Ratio

Waist-to-hip ratio is a measurement for determining your fat distribution and therefore your level of risk for developing heart disease, high blood pressure, or diabetes.

1. Measure in inches your waist (the smallest measurement below your ribcage and above your navel) and hips (the largest measurement around the widest part of your buttocks), and record those results.

Waist: _____ Hips: _____

2. Divide your waist measurement (W) by your hip measurement (H).

Waist-to-hip ratio (W/H): _____

For men, a ratio of more than .90 indicates an "apple" shape and a higher risk. A ratio of less than .90 indicates a "pear" shape and a lower risk. For women, a ratio of more than .80 indicates an "apple" shape and a higher risk. A ratio of less than .80 indicates a "pear" shape and a lower risk. Enter your waist-to-hip ratio on the form provided at the end of this chapter (p. 114).

Fitness Goal Setting

The goal of any personal fitness plan is to improve overall health, but you may have other, more-specific goals as well. The long-range goal for your own personal fitness plan might be to improve your officiating performance as a result of your improved ability to move efficiently and with greater endurance. Given the results of your personal self-assessment, what are your own goals for each of the four components of health-related physical fitness? To achieve these goals, set short-term targets for the specific areas of fitness that you want to improve. Complete the columns labeled "short-term goal" and "target date" on the form provided at the end of this chapter. Reward yourself for adopting healthy lifestyle behaviors with small incentives that motivate you to keep working toward your long-term goals.

Reevaluate your goals as your fitness improves. Keep track of your progress by periodically re-taking the self-assessment tests. With success, continue to set reasonable, short-term goals, and reward yourself as you work to accomplish them.

Your Physical Workout

Your selection of physical activities directly affects your chance for success. A physically active lifestyle offers incredible health benefits if participation is regular, preferably daily. Making physical activity and healthy eating a daily habit are the keys to true health and wellness. As you plan your physical workout, keep in mind that you will be much more likely to work out regularly if you select activities that you enjoy and that are convenient for you. Also keep in mind the sport-specific activities suggested in table 8.1.

These are the four components of your physical workout:

1. *Warm-up and stretching exercises.* These exercises raise your body's temperature in an effort to prepare it for physical activity. After your body's temperature is raised, a series of stretching exercises further help to prepare it for activity and reduce the chance of injury.

2. *Cardiorespiratory endurance activities.* These aerobic-type (long-duration and lower-intensity) activities are geared to raise your heart rate for a prolonged period and force your body to become more efficient at transporting oxygen to the working muscles.

3. *Muscular fitness activities.* These anaerobic-type (or short-duration and explosive-intensity) activities are geared to enhance your body's ability to respond powerfully through the adaptation

of the muscular system to some weight-bearing stress.

4. *Cool-down and stretching exercises.* In contrast to the warm-up, the cool-down prepares your body to finish activity through the gentle lowering of body temperature.

Warm-Up and Stretching Activities

Begin your warm-up by walking for five to seven minutes, gradually increasing your pace until you begin a slow jog. You can also jump rope, cycle, or do another total-body activity, starting at a low intensity and gradually increasing to a moderate intensity for a total of five to seven minutes. After warming up, complete some or all of the stretching exercises starting on page 105, holding each position about 15 seconds and repeating each stretch three to five times.

Cardiorespiratory Endurance Activities

Once your body has warmed up and you have completed your flexibility exercises, you can begin the cardiorespiratory endurance portion of your workout. If you are just beginning an exercise program or resuming exercise after a long lay-off, start your first week by walking briskly 12 to 15 minutes per day. A good rule of thumb suggests that you should add no more than 20 percent to the duration of your activity each week. Thus, within a few weeks of beginning a new program, you can increase your time up to 20 or 30 minutes, but you will have gradually accomplished that goal rather than attempting to meet it within a few days. If you have stayed reasonably active in your off-season, a 15-minute walk may seem a waste of time. We caution you, however, to resist that urge that suggests you could run five to eight miles over your lunch hour with ease and still have time to get a sandwich or two. Allow your body to adjust gradually to your more physically active lifestyle, and it will reward you with fewer injuries and more officiating enjoyment.

Depending on the sport you officiate, you should consider adding sport-specific movements as the season draws nearer. If you are physically active and in good condition, now you

Table 8.1 Sport-Specific Fitness Activities

Sample sports	Recommended off-season activities	Recommended in-season activities
Basketball	Longer duration (>20 min.) running cycling, and swimming to develop cardiorespiratory (aerobic) fitness base: • 3–5 times per week • Focus on running because of sport demands Overall body weight training to improve muscle fitness: • 2–3 times per week • Focus particularly on lower body because of sport demands Overall body flexibility routine: • 5–7 times per week • Focus primarily on lower body	Maintain aerobic base, but add short duration, more explosive movements (anaerobic) for preseason and in-season: • Sport-specific movements such as sliding, backward running, and forward running • 3–4 times per week in preseason; 1–2 times per week in-season Depending on how many games are officiated per week, use day after game as a rest day, then begin weekly workouts after rest.
Baseball and softball	Longer duration (>20 min.) walking, running, cycling, and swimming to develop cardiorespiratory (aerobic) fitness base: • 3–5 times per week • Primarily for overall health, so adding longer walks (40+ minutes) can improve overall health and help reduce weight. Overall body weight training to improve muscle fitness: • 2–3 times per week • Include focus on abdominal muscles to reduce chance of lower back injury. Overall body flexibility routine: • 5–7 times per week	Maintain aerobic base, but add extensive flexibility routine for lower body (especially those umpires working primarily behind the plate).

(continued)

Table 8.1 *Continued*

Sample sports	Recommended off-season activities	Recommended in-season activities
Football	Longer duration (>20 min.) running cycling, and swimming to develop cardiorespiratory (aerobic) fitness base: • 3–5 times per week • Focus on running because of sport demands • Cross train with stationary cycling, cross country skiing, and jumping rope. Overall body weight training to improve muscle fitness: • 2–3 times per week • Focus particularly on lower body because of sport demands Overall body flexibility routine: • 5–7 times per week • Focus primarily on lower body	Add short duration, more explosive movements (anaerobic) for pre-season and in-season: • Sport-specific movements such as sliding, backward running, and forward running to mark a downfield spot • 3–4 times per week in pre-season; 1–2 times per week in-season Because typically games are played toward the end of the week and on weekends, plan to rest on Sunday or Monday, then begin weekly workouts on Tuesday with light running/walking.
Soccer, lacrosse, and field hockey	Longer duration (>20 min.) running, cycling, and swimming to develop cardiorespiratory (aerobic) fitness base: • 3–5 times per week • Focus on running because of sport demands Overall body weight training to improve muscle fitness: • 2–3 times per week • Include focus on lower body because of sport demands Overall body flexibility routine: • 5–7 times per week • Focus primarily on lower body	Maintain aerobic base, but add short duration, more explosive movements (anaerobic) movements for pre-season and in-season: • Sport-specific movements such as sliding, backward running, and forward running with rapid changes in direction. • 3–4 times per week in pre-season; 1–2 times per week in-season Depending on how many games are officiated per week, use day after game as a rest day, then begin weekly workouts after rest.

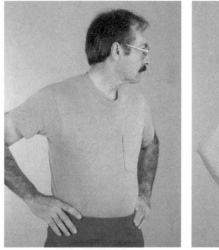

Head turn (left): turn your head slowly to look over one shoulder, then the other.

Head lean (right): keeping your shoulders relaxed, lean your head toward one shoulder, then the other.

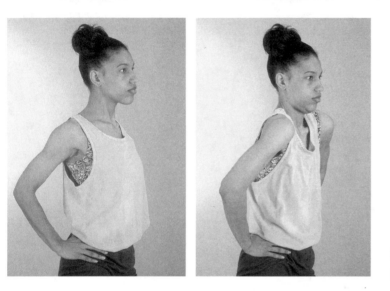

Shoulder rolls. With your hands on your hips, gently rotate both shoulders at once.

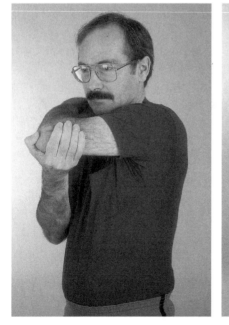

Shoulder stretch (left): use your right arm to gently pull your left elbow across your chest, and vice versa.

Shoulder turn (right): with your hands on your knees, slowly turn your upper body left, then right.

Triceps stretch. Place your left hand between your shoulder blades, as shown. Use your right arm to gently push up and back at your left elbow, then switch sides.

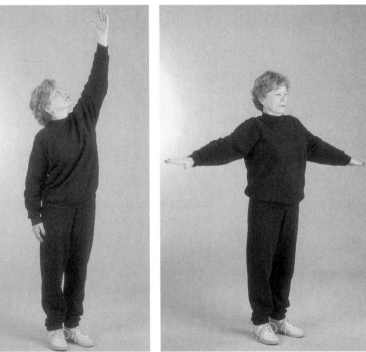

Side reach (left): reach up, not over, with one arm at a time.

Arm circles (right): slowly circle both arms at once, rotating gently at the shoulder.

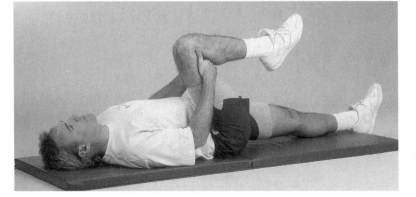

Single knee to chest. Place your hands on back of one knee and pull your knee toward your chest. Do for both legs.

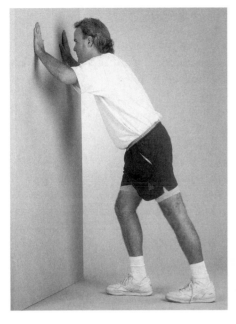

Wall lean (left): keeping your back heel on the ground, turn your foot slightly inward. Do for both sides.

Quadriceps stretch (right): use your left hand to raise your left foot toward your bottom. Switch and do right side as well.

Lunge (left): with both your feet pointing forward, stretch forward on one leg, as shown. Your front knee should be over your front toe.

Hamstring stretch (right): keeping both knees bent slightly, lean over front toe. Perform on both sides.

Butterfly. Holding the soles of your feet together, gently lean forward and hold.

can reflect on the key movements that you perform in your officiating duties and find ways to mirror those movements in your workout. You might, for example, practice sliding sideways and changing directions quickly to simulate the change of possession in football, basketball, or soccer. Although physical agility depends less on cardiorespiratory endurance and more on balance, strength, and power, your overall physical conditioning will help you perform these officiating movements easily through the entire game.

Muscular Fitness Activities

After completing some endurance activity, you should complete a series of muscular fitness activities to enhance your overall physical conditioning. Complete 10 to 12 repetitions of some or all of the following exercises.

Photos on pages 105–110 are from *The ACSM Fitness Book*, 2nd edition, 1998, pages 72–85. Used with permission of Human Kinetics.

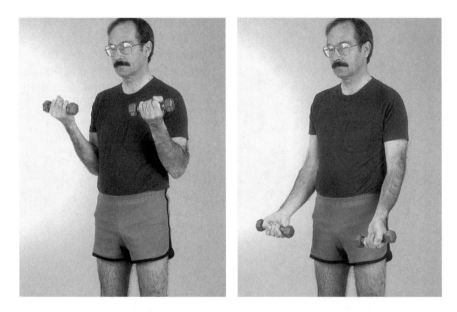

Biceps curls. Bending at the elbow, lift weights toward your shoulders, then lower back to your side.

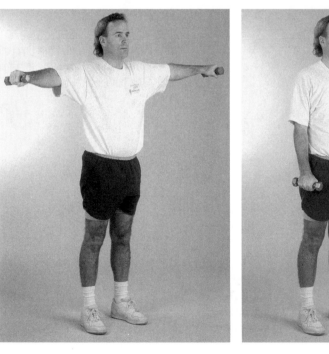

Lateral raises. Keeping your elbows slightly bent, lift weights out to either side, then slowly drop arms back to original position.

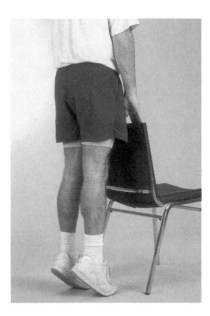

Toe raises. Using the back of a chair for stability, rise up on your toes, then slowly lower your heels back to the floor.

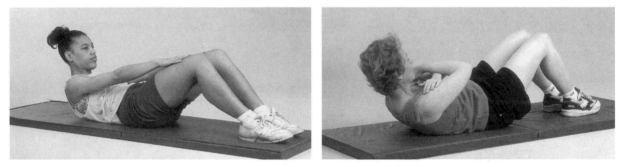

Abdominal crunch (straight-arm, left; crossed arm, right): lift shoulders off the floor until you feel a mild tension in your abdominals. Hold for a few seconds, then return to original position and repeat.

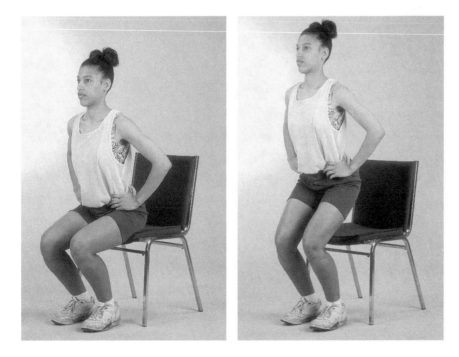

Half squat. Sit at the edge of a chair with your heels under the seat, as shown. Keeping your knees bent, stand without leaning forward.

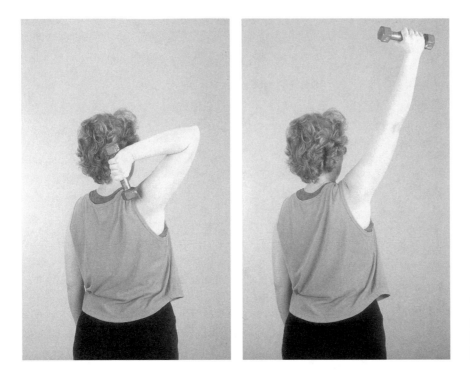

Triceps extension. From the start position at left, raise the weight to the full extension of your arm, then return and repeat.

Standard push-up (on knees or toes): keeping your back straight and your palms flat on the floor, fully extend your arms, hold briefly, then lower yourself back toward the floor.

Cool-Down and Stretching Activities

Following the muscular fitness phase of your workout, it is time to cool down by relaxing and completing the same 10 flexibility exercises you performed as part of your initial warm-up and stretching period. Cooling down allows your heart rate and breathing to resume normal rates. Stretching at the end of a workout helps to ease delayed muscle soreness.

Treating Injuries

Injuries are best avoided by being involved in a well-planned, year-round fitness program. The easiest way to prevent injury is to prepare the body for the activity that it will undertake. Weakness, poor flexibility, imbalance among muscle groups, and lack of endurance can lead to acute or chronic injuries.

To prevent injuries, it is important for you to listen to the signals your body gives. Do not ignore these signals. Symptoms such as pain, tightness, swelling, and spasm are often precursors to serious injury. Knowing when these symptoms begin and end during activity is important in identifying the type and severity of injury. Do they begin while warming up, during activity, or after activity? Do you notice a change when you run harder? Do you notice any difference in symptoms when officiating at night or in a colder environment?

Injuries are classified as acute (sudden-onset) or chronic (overuse). Acute injuries occur suddenly and include sprains, strains, dislocations, fractures, contusions, abrasions, and lacerations. Chronic injuries occur from overuse and are caused by muscle imbalance, poor muscle fitness, poor flexibility, poor cardiorespiratory fitness, improper equipment, or inadequate rehabilitation following a prior injury. Chronic injuries include tendonitis and stress fractures.

Management of an acute injury requires immediate care to control pain, internal and external bleeding, and swelling. This immediate care is important in reducing the severity of the injury and preventing complications. Immediate care includes the RICE method of treatment: rest, ice, compression, and elevation. Ice should be placed directly over the injured site, compression should be applied over the ice, and the injured part should be elevated above the heart. The RICE treatment should be carried out for 24 to 72 hours. The injury should be evaluated and diagnosed as early as possible to determine the type and severity of the injury and to allow treatment to begin quickly.

Acute injuries most common to officials include sprains, strains, and contusions. A sprain is an injury to a ligament (ligaments connect bone to bone), a strain is an injury to the muscle fibers or tendon (tendons connect muscles to bone), and a contusion is the injury of tissue below the skin when it is struck with enough force to crush it.

When to Come Back

When should an official return to activity following an injury? This decision should be made only after knowing how the injury occurred and how severe it is. Medical professionals trained in treating sports-related injuries can be of great assistance when making the decision. The following five criteria can help determine whether return to activity can be done safely:

1. There is no significant pain in the body part.
2. There is normal range of motion.
3. There is no significant swelling.
4. The injured part has at least 90 percent of the strength of the uninjured part.
5. Activities related to officiating can be performed without pain or limping.

Sprains

The management of sprains depends on the severity of the injury. Sprains are graded as follows: Grade I, the ligament is stretched but not torn; grade II, the ligament is partially torn with increased laxity of the joint; grade III, the ligament is completely torn with instability of the joint. The most common sprains among officials involve the ligaments of the ankle and knee.

Grade I sprains are treated with rest, ice, compression, and elevation. Grade II sprains are treated with rest, ice, compression, elevation, and immobilization of the joint. Grade III sprains are treated with rest, ice, compression, elevation, prolonged immobilization of the joint, and possible surgery. Immobilization of the joint should be controlled by medical professionals. Immobilization may be only partial to allow some joint movement. Return to activity is determined using the criteria previously outlined.

Strains

Strains are also managed according to the severity of the injury. Muscle strains are classified as mild, moderate, and severe. Mild and moderate strains are differentiated by the amount of pain, weakness, and spasm involved with the injury. Severe strains can involve an actual defect in the muscle, including complete rupture of tendons such as the Achilles and patellar (thigh–to–knee-cap) tendons. Common strains in officiating involve the hamstring, quadriceps, hip adductor (muscles that draw the legs together), and calf muscles.

Mild strains are treated with rest, ice, compression, and elevation. Moderate strains are treated with rest, ice, compression, elevation, and possibly immobilization. Severe strains are treated with rest, ice, compression, elevation, immobilization, and possibly surgery. Return to activity is determined as previously outlined.

Contusions

Contusions usually occur when an official collides with a participant or falls onto the playing surface. Contusions may be superficial and involve only tissues near the skin, or they may involve deeper muscle tissue, with increased internal bleeding that causes a hematoma (a swelling that contains blood).

Specific Common Injuries

In the following sections, we discuss the treatment and management of some injuries common to officials. Before an official undertakes any treatment, a qualified medical professional should examine and diagnose the injury.

Ankle Sprains

The highest percentage of ankle injuries involve the outside ankle ligaments. Treatment of ankle injuries can be separated into three phases: Phase I begins immediately following the injury, phase II begins when the individual is able to bear weight without increasing pain or swelling, and phase III begins when the individual is able to perform functional exercises.

Phase I consists of treatment with ice, compression, and elevation (see page 111). A brace or taping is used for protection. Weight bearing is encouraged if it can be tolerated, using crutches as needed. Gentle ankle dorsiflexion (flexing the foot upward) and plantar flexion (flexing the foot downward) and isometric exercises are started as soon as possible. These exercises include ankle circles, ankle pumping, and "alphabet writing" with the big toe. Contrast baths can be started 48 to 72 hours after the injury to help decrease swelling.

Phase II begins when the individual can bear weight without increased pain or swelling. Exercises to increase strength and increase the range of motion of the ankle are started in this phase, including dorsiflexion, plantar-flexion, eversion (turning the foot outward), inversion (turning the foot inward), and Achilles tendon–stretching exercises.

Phase III includes functional exercises to increase conditioning, agility, proprioception (sensing internal stimuli), and endurance. A proprioceptive exercise is standing on the injured foot with the eyes closed. Running exercises in this phase include running straight forward, backward, and in increasingly smaller figure 8s.

The three-phase treatment program takes from 10 days to two weeks for minor sprains up to six to eight weeks for severe sprains. The use of ankle taping or a brace to protect the injured ankle should be considered when initially returning to regular activities.

Calf Strains

Calf strains usually involve the inside head of the gastrocnemius (calf) muscle. The initial evaluation determines the severity of the injury to rule out the possibility of injury to the Achilles tendon.

Initial treatment includes ice, compression, and elevation to control bleeding and swelling. The injured person may need crutches to reduce pain while walking. Elevating the heel by using a heel lift in the shoe relieves stretching of the muscle while walking and during stretching and strengthening exercises of the gastrocnemius muscle. Exercises include towel stretches, gastrocnemius stretches with the knee straight and bent, plantar-flexion exercises using surgical tubing, and later toe raises with weight as tolerated. The injured person should be able to tolerate functional exercises, including running forward, backward, and in figure 8s, before returning to normal activity.

Achilles Tendon Strain

Injury to the Achilles tendon can include partial to full rupture of the tendon. It is important to differentiate between an Achilles tendon strain and a gastrocnemius (calf) strain. If pain or tenderness begins in the Achilles tendon (tendinitis), it is important to begin treatment early to prevent progression to partial or full tendon rupture. See a doctor to determine which strain you are experiencing. Exercise and management are similar to those for calf strains.

Plantar Fasciitis

Plantar fasciitis is pain in the sole of the foot near the heel where the plantar fascia (a sheet of connective tissue that covers the sole of the foot) attaches to the heel bone. Treatment includes the use of an orthotic for support of the arch of the foot and a heel pad. Stretching the plantar fascia and the Achilles tendon is important. Ice and contrast baths can also be used to relieve symptoms. Normal activities can generally be resumed within six to eight weeks.

Shin Splints

Shin splints is the name used to describe several conditions that cause chronic lower-leg pain. The pain can be caused by stress fractures, compartment syndrome (enlargement and compression of the muscles in the lower leg that can impede blood flow and cause cramps), and posterior tibial syndrome. It is important that a medical professional make a correct diagnosis so that the correct treatment can begin as soon as possible.

Stress Fractures

The most common stress fractures for officials are those in the tibia and fibula, the two bones of the lower leg. Stress fractures occur when repeated stress on a bone causes a disruption, or fracture, of the bone. Stress fractures are often so thin that X rays may not reveal them initially; other tests may be required to determine if a stress fracture is present. Weight bearing causes pain, which usually increases with running and jumping activities. Treatment includes reduction of activity. Officiating activities should be avoided for four to six weeks. Crutches are necessary only when walking causes pain.

Posterior Tibial Syndrome

Posterior tibial syndrome is caused by repetitive motions or a mechanical misalignment of the foot. Pain is usually felt along the inside edge of the shinbone just below the knee. A medical professional should evaluate the injury to determine whether orthotics are necessary to correct the alignment of the foot. Treatment includes reducing activities, wearing soft-soled shoes, and stretching and strengthening exercises of the gastrocnemius and posterior tibial muscles of the calf. Ice and contrast baths are also used to relieve symptoms.

Anterior Compartment Syndrome

Compartment syndrome is pain that occurs when the muscles in an enclosed compartment of the body enlarge due to the increased circulation that occurs with activity. The anterior (front) muscle compartment of the lower leg includes the tibialis anterior, extensor hallucis longus, and extensor muscles of the toes, which are enclosed by the bones of the lower leg and a sheet of connective tissue. Because muscle and nerve damage can occur if this syndrome is not treated, a correct diagnosis and prompt treatment are very important. Treatment should include close observation by medical professionals and may include surgery to relieve symptoms.

Low-Back Strains and Sprains

Low-back strains are injuries that involve the muscles of the low back; low-back sprains are injuries that involve the ligaments of the low back. Pain in the low back area can radiate into the buttocks. Pain usually increases with activity, so see a medical professional before you work another game. A doctor should diagnose the injury to rule out a herniated disk or other nerve damage. Treatment includes the use of heat or cold to relieve pain and spasm along with exer-

cises to increase range of motion and strength in the low back.

Summary

The three steps in designing a personal fitness plan are self-assessment, goal setting, and selection of physical activities. Self-assessment helps you determine your current fitness levels and set realistic fitness goals. You can then select activities to help you achieve your goals. Your physical fitness plan should include four key components: a warm-up and stretching period, cardiorespiratory endurance activity, muscular fitness activity, and a cool-down and stretching period. The final step in maintaining your health and fitness is learning to avoid, recognize, and get appropriate medical treatment for injuries.

Self-Assessment and Goal-Setting Form

Use this form to record your current fitness level and set your personal goals. Review information in chapter 3 to help you set attainable, measurable goals. Make copies of the form and periodically record your fitness scores to check your progress and reassess your goals. Note that maintenance can be a goal for you if you are already pleased with your current performance.

Name: _____ Date: _____ Age: _____ Weight: _____	Current score	ACSM fitness level category	Short-term goal	Target date
Cardiorespiratory fitness • *1–Mile walk*	Time: _____ Heart rate: _____ $\dot{V}O_2$max: _____		Time: _____ Heart rate: _____ $\dot{V}O_2$max: _____	
Muscular fitness • *Push-ups*				
Flexibility • *Sit-and-reach*	_____ inches		_____ inches	
Body composition • *Body mass index*				
Body composition • *Waist-to-hip ratio*				

Part IV
....

Managing Professional Responsibilities

9

Understanding Your Legal Responsibilities

Mel Narol

In this chapter you'll learn

- how the judicial system rules on officials' game calls,
- that officials are viewed as independent contractors,
- about player injuries for which officials may be liable, and
- about players' rights that must be protected.

Sometimes legal issues affect sports officiating, either in terms of rulings made by officials or in regard to the rights of people engaged in athletics. As rule enforcers, officials are sometimes challenged severely, and on occasion courts have been asked to overrule officials' decisions. The courts have seldom overturned their judgment calls that have taken place in sports.

Officials, on the other hand, must be conscious of players' rights too. Specifically, they must take precautions to guard player safety, and officials must also recognize when conditions arise that might threaten the civil rights of participants. In addition, officials should have their own medical insurance if they are injured while officiating, because courts have generally decided that they cannot be covered for workers' compensation by an organization that hires them. Officials in some states are covered by a blanket policy for injuries sustained while officiating and for liability about their decisions, but not every state is enrolled in this program, which is administered by the National Federation of State High School Associations. It is also possible to obtain automatic coverage for injuries and liability (plus other things such as loss of game stipends due to injury) by joining the National Association of Sports Officials (see chapter 12 and Appendix A).

Judicial Review of Officials' Game Calls

Courts have uniformly determined in every reported decision that sports officials' game calls cannot be challenged by disgruntled teams, players, or fans where a sports official has made an error in judgment or misapplied a game rule. Disagreement over a call is part of the game and should remain on the court, not *in* court. There is no legal claim for judicial review of a sports official's honest judgmental error or misapplication of a rule during a game unless there is demonstrable bad faith or corruption.

Judgment Calls

The genesis for the courts' view that sports officials' judgment calls are not subject to judicial review was the 1945 New York City Municipal Court case of *Shapiro v. Queens County Jockey Club*. In that case, only three of the six gates opened at the start of a horse race. The starter signaled an assistant a short distance down the track, who waved his recall flag. All the horses stopped, except a horse called Breezing Home. Breezing Home ran around the track for the full distance of the race and crossed the finish line. The race officials confirmed that it had been a false start.

A short while later, the race was run again and was won by another horse; Breezing Home finished fifth among the six horses. The plaintiff in the court case, who had bet on Breezing Home to win, argued that the first running of the race was an official race and that he should be paid his share of the winners' pool. He questioned the decisions of the starter and the race officials. There was no proof that Breezing Home would have won if the false start had been a fair start.

Relying on the fact that horse racing is governed by the rules of the State Racing Commission and the race track, the court decided that judges should not substitute their determination "for that of those persons who were actually there at the time and who were specifically charged with the duty of determining the winners." When the officials declared a false start in the race, the court emphasized, "the plaintiff was bound by said decision. There was only one official race."

The court thus established a rule that has withstood analysis for more than 50 years and has become the general rule regarding officials of all sports.

In all competitive sports, it is important to have umpires, referees, timekeepers, and other officials who are experienced, mentally alert, fair, and otherwise well-qualified to make immediate decisions and whose decisions must be final and binding. Officials are truly judges of facts because they are closer to the actual situation and people involved. Courts have found that on-site officials' immediate reactions and decisions during the conduct of the sport should receive greater credence and consideration than the remote observation by a court during litigation instigated by a disgruntled participant or spectator.

In 1953 in *Tilelli v. Christenberry*, a trial judge in the Supreme Court of New York upheld the decision of a professional boxing referee and a ringside judge. The match lasted the scheduled 10 rounds; then the referee and one judge cast their votes for boxer Giardella, while the third judge voted for boxer Graham. As a result of this 2–1 vote, Giardella was declared the winner. Later, the New York State Athletic Commission, of which two members attended the match, changed the voting card for two rounds of the judge who had voted for Giardella. This decision was based on Giardella's failure to follow certain rules and a suspicion that he was involved in a betting scheme. Boxer Graham was therefore awarded the decision. Giardella then filed a lawsuit. The court found that the commission's suspicion was insufficient to change the outcome. The court determined that the judge's vote should not have been changed because a court should not substitute its judgment for that of a boxing judge and stated, "[I]t is the essence of enjoyment of a sporting spectacle that the decision follow the event immediately."

The Supreme Court of New Hampshire in 1982 in *Snow v. New Hampshire Interscholastic Athletic Association* dealt with a challenge by a high school track star who participated in the 800-meter event in a state athletic association track meet. Plaintiff Snow alleged that he was one of the event leaders when he was cut off and physically brushed by another runner, resulting in his finishing seventh and failing to qualify for the

Officials judge the acts of players, and they interpret what those acts indicate. To date, no court has overturned an official's judgment call about a game situation.

statewide Meet of Champions. No track official was located near the spot where the alleged incident occurred. Consequently, when the plaintiff filed a protest with the meet director, the director could not change the race result because he had no official's report. Snow filed a lawsuit to allow him to run in the Meet of Champions, and the trial court ruled for Snow. The Supreme Court then reversed the trial court's ruling, saying "the role of courts in this area [judicial scrutiny of a sports official's decision] is exceedingly limited and we [do] not intend to merge the stadium bench with the judicial bench."

In *Bain v. Gillispie* in 1984, the Iowa Court of Appeals was faced with a claim by a merchandise company that a college sports official had made an incorrect game call, leading to lost sales of the company's products emblazoned with the losing team's logo. Jim Bain was a veteran college basketball referee working a 1982 Big Ten Conference men's game between the University of Iowa and Purdue University. Near the end of the game, he determined that an Iowa player committed a foul, enabling a Purdue player to shoot two free throws that resulted in Purdue winning the game. Following the game, the

Gillispies, whose company was located in Iowa, began to sell T-shirts bearing a likeness of Bain with a rope around his neck and captioned "Jim Bain Fan Club." Bain filed for an injunction to stop the shirts from being sold and for monetary damages. In response, the Gillispies filed a counterclaim alleging that Bain's call was negligent and damaged their business, including the sale of items with the Iowa logo on them, because of Iowa's failure to advance to the national tournament. The Gillispies claimed that Bain made a judgmental error. The trial court granted Bain's motion for summary judgment and dismissed the Gillispies' counterclaim without a trial.

The court of appeals, relying in part on the National Association of Sports Officials' friend of the court brief on behalf of all sports officials, affirmed the dismissal of the counterclaim. It decided that a sports official owes no legal duty to a merchandiser for game calls. As in prior cases, the court reasoned that, in the absence of bad faith or corruption, a sports official's judgment-based game call is not subject to judicial review. The court adopted the strong policy considerations eloquently expressed by the Iowa trial court:

This is a case where the undisputed facts are of such a nature that a rational fact finder could only reach one conclusion—no foreseeability, no duty, no liability. Heaven knows what uncharted morass a court would find itself in if it were to hold that an athletic official subjects himself to liability every time he might make a questionable call. The possibilities are mind boggling. If there is a liability to a merchandiser like the Gillispies, why not to the thousands upon thousands of Iowa fans who bleed Hawkeye black and gold every time the whistle blows? It is bad enough when Iowa loses without transforming a loss into a litigation field day for "Monday morning quarterbacks."

A recent case in Pennsylvania, *Pagnotta v. Pennsylvania Interscholastic Athletic Association*, involved a high school wrestler, Randy Pagnotta, who was disqualified for allegedly illegally striking his opponent during a state tournament match. Pagnotta claimed that he should not have been disqualified by the referee because a similar incident had occurred in another match not involving him on the same day and the other wrestler was not disqualified. The state wrestling rules provided for disqualification for intentionally striking an opponent and also stated, "On matters of judgment the referee shall have full control of the match and his decision shall be final."

Though wrestler Randy Pagnotta was able to convince a judge that the referee had erred and was granted permission to wrestle in the next round, an appeals court immediately reversed the first judge's decision, citing the prior precedent of nonintervention by courts regarding judgment calls by an official. Pagnotta thus did not wrestle again in the state tournament.

Rule Calls

The principle that a sports official's game calls are outside the jurisdiction of the courts was applied by the Supreme Court of Georgia in 1981 in a case involving a high school football referee who admitted that he misapplied a rule. In *Georgia High School Association v. Waddell*, the court ruled that it did not possess authority to review the call of a high school football referee.

In a pre-state play-off football game between Osborne and Lithia Springs High Schools, Osborne had the ball and was ahead 7-6, with approximately seven minutes remaining in the game. On fourth down and 21 yards to go, Osborne punted, but a penalty for roughing the kicker was called on Lithia Springs. The referee assessed a 15-yard penalty but incorrectly declared that it was again fourth down with six yards to go. By rules, Osborne should have been awarded an automatic first down also. Osborne punted again, and Lithia Springs drove down the field to score a field goal. Later in the game, Lithia Springs scored again and won the game 16-7.

Osborne sued, and its cause was upheld by a local court, but within a few days that decision was reversed by the Supreme Court of Georgia. The court refused to review the referee's call, even though the referee made an error regarding a rule, declaring itself "without authority to review decisions of football referees, because those decisions do not represent judicial controversies."

Bad Faith or Corruption

It has been rare in sports history for sports officials to act in bad faith or through corruption to influence the outcome of a contest. But in cases of bad faith or corruption, courts may intercede to correct the intentional wrong. Like the horse-racing case that set the legal precedent for not overturning sports officials' judgment calls, another horse-racing case set the precedent for the court's handling of corruption cases. In the 1897 case of *Wellington v. Monroe Trotting Park Co.*, the Supreme Judicial Court of Maine declared several racing judges guilty of illegal behavior for deciding before a race to award a certain horse first place, when in fact another horse beat it to the wire. In this case the court demonstrated a willingness to overturn officials' decisions because the officials were guilty of willfully influencing a contest, which could erode the public's confidence in the integrity of sports officials.

Officials' Employment Status

California baseball umpire Stan Feigenbaum turned to the state for help when he was struck in the head by a throw in 1974. The boy who threw the ball had no liability insurance, and the California Umpires Association did not have workers' compensation insurance either. Feigenbaum filed a claim with the California Workers' Compensation Uninsured Employers' Fund, a state resource for injured employees. He was unsuccessful in his plea, because an independent contractor is not eligible for workers' compensation.

The question of sports officials' status as employees or independent contractors has been debated for over three decades. Courts have generally found officials not to be employees, making employee benefits unavailable to them. Such decisions by state courts establish precedents that other states follow. Local officiating associations, school districts, and even state high school associations are not considered employers of sports officials, meaning they have no obligation to maintain workers' compensation insurance for sports officials.

The general test to determine whether a sports official is an employee or an independent contractor rests on whether the hiring entity has the right to control the official's performance. Basically, an organization that hires an official controls only the fact that the official be present and perform according to a standard that is not set by the contracting agent.

High School Districts Are Not Employers

Beginning in 1956, state courts in almost every case have found that a school district is not the official's employer for workers' compensation purposes. In 1977 the New Jersey Appellate Di-

In today's world, gender equity, independent contractor status, and legal liability are just some of the issues faced by officials and by those who use their services.

vision decided against a high school basketball official's claim for compensation when he injured his teeth in a game. The court based its decision on the fact that the official had another full-time job and that he worked for numerous schools. Courts have also used the facts that officials furnish their own equipment and that no tax is withheld from their stipends as reasons to deny claims and to reaffirm officials' status as independent contractors.

Officials' Associations Are Not Employers

In 1973 a Maryland court decided that an injured umpire was not employed by his association. Umpire Donald Gale had been struck by a player with his bat in the hip, neck, and leg. In its judgment the court decided that, because Gale was not obliged to accept every assignment and could turn back games once they were assigned, he was indeed operating independently.

State High School Associations Are Not Employers

An Arizona wrestler, injured in a match, sued the referee and the state athletic association, and the state eventually settled the claim out of court. The referee, however, instead of settling, sought to demonstrate that the state was the responsible employer. An Arizona appeals court determined in 1992 that the state association was not the official's employer. The short duration of work, limited control by the employer, and one-time method of payment for specific services were all factors in the court's decision.

The state of Alaska once presented an umpire's association in Anchorage with a substantial bill for unemployment compensation insurance, but the Department of Labor determined that the association was not a liable employer, thus relieving the group of the insurance obligation.

College Conferences Are Not Employers

Although college conferences sometimes have a staff of officials, no workers' compensation decisions have held them responsible when officials make claims for injury. By and large, officials must secure their own accident and medical insurance.

Officials filed an unfair labor practice claim with the National Labor Relations Board because the Big East Conference would not bargain with the Collegiate Basketball Officials Association over pay scales. Again, the issue of officials having other full-time jobs was a guiding factor in the denial of an appeal.

Liability of Officials for Player Injuries

Officials must be sure that a game is played according to the rules and that rough and illegal play are properly penalized. Officials can be held liable for injuries that result from repeated fouls that they fail to call. Baiting and taunting that precipitate a fight can also be considered negligence if officials did not take action to curb the undesirable conduct.

The role of a sports official docs not include administering first aid, unless a life-threatening situation exists. When a player is injured during a game, officials should follow these steps:

1. Stop the game as soon as possible.
2. Report the injury to the player's coach.

The Issue of Neutrality

Pennsylvania football referee George Lynch lost an appeal for benefits in 1989 after he tore a calf muscle near the end of a high school game. The injury led to complications that resulted in the amputation of Lynch's leg below the knee. Control over Lynch's activities during a game was the key issue in the case, and the court decided that if a hiring organization tried to control an official's game performance, "the issue of *neutrality,* which is the hallmark of being independent, would be compromised."

Rained *In*?

Indoor venues are not exempt from weather problems. In January 1986, NBA referee Mike Mathis halted a game at Seattle in the first half due to rain leaking onto the playing surface. A 1997 college basketball game at Walsh College in Ohio was terminated with 18 minutes remaining because of condensation forming on the playing floor, which was made of a plastic-foam composite. The humid atmosphere in the gym combined with frigid conditions outdoors to create an exceptionally slippery floor. A game administrator helped the officials arrive at the decision to call the game off.

3. Notify the game site administrator.

4. Stay near the player only to observe whether the player is conscious, then move aside to permit attendants' access to the player.

5. Permit other personnel to handle the injury and to move the player as necessary.

6. Hold up the game until the injured player is pronounced ready to play by authorized personnel or is removed from the area. (In some sports, players who are rendered unconscious via play action may not reenter the game without a doctor's permission.)

7. Be patient; in many circumstances it may be necessary to wait for medical attendants to arrive and make decisions about removing the injured player.

Duty to Enforce Sport Safety Rules

Safety rules regarding game equipment are spelled out in each sport's rule publications. For example, metal standards such as volleyball-net supports and football goalposts may need to be padded. Concrete hazards such as curbs and shot-put berms may need to be padded to avoid negligence when a field hockey, soccer, or football game is to be played. Player equipment also is subject to stringent specifications. Only certain kinds of footwear are permitted in each sport, and protective padding is defined by the rules, including the necessary width of slow-recovery absorbent materials. Mouth guards and kneepads are sometimes required. Certain kinds of support braces for leg joints may be permitted. Officials must know all these requirements then inspect

the site and the players to be sure of compliance. Overlooking vital equipment and its protective dimensions may mean that an official could be held liable for negligence in an injury case.

Duty to Confirm Safe Weather Conditions

A Superior Court of New Jersey lawsuit involved a football player who became partially paralyzed when he fractured two vertebrae while trying to make a tackle. The player's suit, which named three high school football officials, among others, claimed that the field was unsafe due to heavy rains. The suit against the officials was dismissed. The court found that the officials controlled the game properly and did not make mistakes in judgment about the field conditions. But a similar case involving an injured football player and a rain-soaked field in Wisconsin was settled out of court; the officials were part of the settling group because they were found to be negligent in allowing the game to be played.

Inclement weather conditions can give rise to liability claims against sports officials. Officials have a duty to be sure that weather conditions are safe for play, and if weather deteriorates during a game—particularly if lightning starts—officials should err on the side of caution and insist that players leave the premises for their safety.

Duty to Properly Inspect the Playing Surface

Rules impose an obligation on officials to note visible hazards—whether natural or artificial—and have them corrected before games. Natural hazards include pitted fields, rocks, or mud holes. Artificial hazards include protruding sprinkler

Safety Check

In Oakland, California, a softball player injured herself while stepping into a depression near home plate and sued the umpire, the city, and the local athletic district, alleging that the umpire failed to correct the field condition and that the umpire's association had neglected to train the umpire to deal with field safety conditions. In this case, the player lost the suit, but the umpire might well have been negligent if in fact he or she did not look for or notice the depression by the plate or, if he or she *had* noticed the depression but did not have it taken care of. The key point is that officials need to assure the safety of the playing field or court or else risk a lawsuit.

heads, protruding drainage conduits, curbing too close to the playing field, concrete runways not used in the game being played, goals for sports other than the one being played, debris, and loose bases or faulty pitcher's rubber. If the hazard or hazardous condition cannot be removed or secured, the hazard might be made safe by padding. Taking precautions will likely absolve an official of negligence. A New Jersey track official was sued for injuries sustained by a high school broad jumper who slipped on a takeoff board. A jury found the official not liable, because the board was not wet from rain or from sprinklers; it was new and shiny with white enamel, meeting specifications for the sport.

Duty to Protect Players' Civil and Religious Rights

Sports officials may also be targets of lawsuits alleging that they violated a player's civil or religious rights. Whether or not yarmulkes (skull caps) worn by Orthodox Jewish players could be secured with hairpins was the problem in a California dispute. State commissioner Dean Crowley ruled that the clips were permissible, even though rules forbade metal objects such as jewelry worn on the head or neck. Game officials previously had given players the option of removing the head coverings or forfeiting a game. Other officials made players remove their yarmulkes halfway through a game.

In a similar Illinois case, a court also ruled that Jewish players must be permitted to wear their skull caps in accordance with religious dictates, but the opinion stipulated, "We are reasonably sure that a secure head covering exists or can be devised at trivial cost without violating any tenet of Orthodox Judaism." A 1992 rules change permits basketball players to wear headpieces if they are "not abrasive, hard, or dangerous to any other player and attached in such a way that it is highly likely they will not come off during play." Plastic, Velcro, double-sticky tape, or elastic bands might be the answer.

Legislative Efforts

The National Association of Sports Officials in 1987 designed limited-liability model legislation to curb the growing number of liability lawsuits against sports officials. The model legislation puts the burden of proof on the plaintiff to show that the official acted with *gross, not ordinary*, negligence. To date, 10 states have adopted legislation based on this model: Arkansas, Georgia, Hawaii, Maryland, Mississippi, Nevada, New Jersey, North Carolina, Ohio, and Tennessee. Legislation is pending in other states.

Summary

Officials may not be aware of how they themselves are legally responsible when they step on a floor or field to work a contest. This chapter spelled out how the judicial system rules on officials' game calls. It also focused on officials' employment status as independent contractors, and liability of officials for player injuries. Now that you know your legal duties as an official, the next chapter will summarize your rights and business responsibilities.

10

Knowing Your Legal Rights and Business Responsibilities

Mel Narol

In this chapter you'll learn

- useful business procedures,

- officials' right to recover damages from game-related injuries,

- officials' right to recover for civil rights violations and discrimination, and

- protective policies for sports officials' associations.

Just as officials need to guard the well-being of players, so too do they need an umbrella of pro-

tection for themselves. First of all, they need to be sound businesspeople, because usually they are in business for themselves. The previous chapter showed the need for officials to carry their own medical and accident insurance. Some state and national officiating organizations have blanket insurance policies available for such eventualities. But officials themselves need to be assured that if circumstances operate against them, opportunities for seeking justice are available. Some states have statutes that are designed to protect officials from physical harm. Officials need to be aware of all avenues for impartial redress. Associations organized for the welfare of officials also need to have formal policies that ensure the fairness of their practices. This chapter explains these vital protective dimensions of athletic officiating.

Independent Contractor Status

As a paid worker, you are essentially in business for yourself. It is important for you to observe the formalities of this setup.

You'll usually be issued a contract for game assignments. This contract is a legal document that assures the assigning authority of your services at a given time and place for a specific sum. If you should fail to fulfill the stipulations of the contract, you may be obliged to pay a penalty, usually a game fee. Often, an individual represents a school or a league in procuring officials, and that individual may send several contracts for games. It is a good business practice to return contracts promptly. You should sign the contract, keep a copy, and send the other copy back to the party who issued the contract. Be informed that when schools are forced to break a contract, they don't always compensate the official, although they should.

Contracts usually indicate who your partners are. The terms may or may not include stipends for meals and mileage, depending on the region where you work and the customary policies of the school. It is important for you to keep a calendar of your officiating obligations, with times and locales clearly delineated. Sometimes officials get mixed up on starting times or cannot find the game site. Tardiness or failure to show up for a scheduled game is damaging to an official's reputation.

Sometimes giving up a game assignment is necessary due to injury, job requirements, or personal emergencies. There is probably a policy in your geographic area for nullifying contracts. It is important for you to learn how to be relieved of an obligation. Often, local groups have a replacement pool and standard practices for obtaining an acceptable substitute. In all cases, though, you are expected to cancel a game only for legitimate reasons, and working an alternate game is ordinarily frowned on as an excuse. Successful officiating rests on your building a reputation for reliability and integrity.

Sometimes payments are made after games, sometimes at the end of a season. Whenever you are paid, you need to keep track of income and expenses for tax purposes. You are obliged to report income, but you can also deduct such expenses as uniform purchases, mileage to games and meetings, clinic fees, and other outlays connected to your officiating. An accountant can tell you which tax deductions are permissible. If you aren't a businessperson in your regular job, you need to become one when you start to officiate.

Officials' Civil Rights

Sports officials have more vigorously asserted their civil rights during the past 20 years. Cases have involved claims under federal and state civil rights and antidiscrimination laws.

Constitutional Rights

The federal civil rights act prohibits wrongful actions by governmental entities. Oklahoma high school basketball referee Stanley Guffey deserves an ovation for standing up for the independence of sports officials.

On February 4, 1992, Officer Eldridge Wyatt was employed by Douglas High School to provide security during its Oklahoma City Conference Basketball Championship game against Star Spencer High School. With a few minutes left in the game, Officer Wyatt observed suspected gang members moving toward the court. Wyatt believed that the game's intensity might provoke a crowd problem. He approached the teams' coaches and asked them to calm their players during the vigorously played game.

Officer Wyatt also went onto the court and advised Guffey that the vigorous play had inflamed the spectators and requested Guffey to "control the game so we can control the crowd." Officer Wyatt ordered Guffey to start calling more fouls. In response, Guffey stated, "I don't know who you are, but you don't have any business out here on the floor." Officer Wyatt then informed Guffey that he was under arrest and escorted him into a separate room away from the basketball court. After a brief period, Guffey was permitted to return and officiated the game to its conclusion.

Guffey filed a lawsuit in the U.S. District Court in Oklahoma alleging that his federal civil rights had been violated because Wyatt's actions constituted an arrest without probable cause and a violation of the Fourth Amendment to the U.S. Constitution. Officer Wyatt applied to the court for dismissal. He argued that he had sufficient probable cause to arrest Guffey because of his failure to obey a lawful request for assistance from a police officer. Maintaining that he reasonably believed that a riot was imminent, Officer Wyatt contended that Guffey's refusal to act impeded Wyatt's ability to control the crowd and was an obstruction of justice under Oklahoma law. Guffey responded that neither the game nor the crowd were particularly unruly. Guffey likened Officer Wyatt's behavior to that of an irate fan and argued that Officer Wyatt never requested assistance but simply directed him to start "calling more fouls."

The Court of Appeals for the Tenth Circuit upheld the federal district court's decision not to dismiss this lawsuit. The court of appeals found that there was clearly a factual dispute which should be left to the determination of a jury.

The case was then tried in the district court, where the jury found in favor of Guffey and awarded him $4,000. The court then ordered, according to federal civil rights law, that most of his attorneys' fees be paid by the defendant.

Regardless of the words used by Officer Wyatt, there does not appear to be justification for a police officer substituting his judgment for that of a game official by requesting the official to call fouls.

Title VII and State Antidiscrimination Laws

Title VII of the federal Civil Rights Act of 1964, other federal laws, and state antidiscrimination laws prohibit discrimination in employment based on certain protected categories, such as age,

race, national origin, gender, and sexual preference.

Two former NFL officials divided $67,500 in back pay after a 1992 settlement reached by the NFL and the federal Equal Employment Opportunity Commission (EEOC). The EEOC, on behalf of ex-officials Jack Fette and Fred Silva, filed an age-bias suit against the NFL. The EEOC said that the NFL "engaged in a policy of closer scrutiny" of the on-field work of officials aged 60 or older than of the work of younger officials and that the NFL forced the older officials to retire or to move to off-field positions.

Peter Quinn, a second-year NBA referee, filed an unsuccessful lawsuit against the NBA, charging it with breach of contract and unfair labor practices. Quinn became an NBA referee in 1989, giving up an 18-year career as a teacher and football coach. For the 1989-90 season, he ranked 52 of 53 NBA referees. He fell to last of 53 in the 1990-91 season, during which he was paid a salary of $42,000. In June 1991, he was fired by the NBA and by the NBA's minor league, the Continental Basketball Association, in which he had worked for six years.

Quinn charged that the NBA failed to provide specific reasons for his dismissal and failed to list the specific criteria involved in its rating system. He sought damages of $925,000 and other costs. Throughout the case, the NBA claimed that its collective-bargaining agreement with the National Association of Basketball Referees, the referees' union, allowed the league not to rehire Quinn due to low ratings and because he was still on probation. In 1992 the New York Supreme Court trial division ruled that the NBA legally did not rehire Quinn.

In 1998, a New York federal district court jury awarded basketball referee Sandra Ortiz-Del Valle $850,000 compensatory and $7 million

A Case of Discrimination

Ben Dreith, a former NFL official, received $165,000 plus legal fees in settlement of a claim he made against the NFL. Dreith asserted that he was fired after the 1990 season because of his age, which was 67. The suit, filed July 25, 1991, claimed that the NFL was guilty of age discrimination against older persons.

punitive damages in her sex discrimination lawsuit against the NBA. Ortiz-Del Valle claimed that the NBA did not hire her to officiate because she is a woman. The NBA appealed the verdict.

Ortiz-Del Valle had officiated in the U.S. Basketball League in 1991, becoming the first woman to officiate any U.S. men's professional basketball game. She alleged that she was in line to be hired by the NBA and was passed over in favor of male officials of lower caliber. The NBA disagreed and argued that she did not possess the qualities to officiate in the NBA. The NBA had never had a female official when the lawsuit was filed, though several months prior to trial, it announced that it had hired its first two female referees: Dee Kantner and Violet Palmer, who were officiating NBA games at the time of the trial.

Americans With Disabilities Act

The Americans With Disabilities Act (ADA) is a federal law that prohibits discrimination against people with disabilities. A person with a disability is defined under the ADA as someone with a physical or mental impairment that substantially limits a major life activity or a person who can be regarded as having an impairment. An impairment includes being HIV positive or having AIDS, a hearing impairment, mental illness, or a physical disability. Pregnancy is not included within the parameters of the ADA but is included in many state antidiscrimination laws.

Although far reaching in its scope, the ADA is applicable only against an employer, which is defined as "a person engaged in an industry affecting commerce who had 15 or more employ-

The Americans With Disabilities Act prohibits discrimination against people with "disabilities," which are defined as "physical or mental impairment that substantially limits a major life activity."

ees for each working day in each of 20 or more calendar weeks in the current or preceding calendar year." Exempted from this definition is a "bona fide private membership club that is exempt from taxation under Section 501(c) of the Internal Revenue Code of 1986." An employee is defined as "an individual employed by an employer."

In 1994, Chief Judge Myron Thompson of the U.S. District Court for the Middle District of Alabama was faced with the issue of whether a local baseball umpires' association was subject to the ADA. Umpire David Jones sued the Southeast Alabama Baseball Umpires Association (SABUA), alleging that he had been discriminated against in his level of assignments because of a leg prosthesis that he wears due to an amputation. Judge Thompson refused to dismiss Jones's claim on summary judgment; the judge disagreed with the association's defense that it was neither an employer nor an employment agency and, therefore, not a "covered entity" under the ADA.

The SABUA supervises the hiring of baseball umpires for high schools in Houston County, Alabama, and the surrounding area. From 1989 to 1992, the SABUA assigned Jones to work high school junior varsity baseball games. Occasionally, he was assigned to work varsity games. In 1992, Jones notified the SABUA that he no longer desired to umpire only junior varsity games, but rather believed that he was good enough to be assigned solely varsity level games. In March 1992, the SABUA informed Jones that they had rejected his request because, due to his leg prosthesis, it believed that he did not have the mobility to umpire effectively on a regular basis at the varsity level. The SABUA further based its determination on its perception that his disability presented a safety problem and potential injury to him and participants in the games in which he would umpire. This defense is based on Title III of the ADA, which provides that a person with a disability can still be discriminated against if that person "poses a direct threat to the health or safety of others." The words "direct threat" are defined as "a significant risk to the health or safety of others that cannot be eliminated by a modification of policies, practices or procedures, or by the provision of auxiliary aides or services." For an association to determine if such a threat

exists, it must make an individualized assessment of the risk posed, the probability of potential injury, and whether reasonable modification can mitigate the risk.

This safety exception was one of the major reasons noted by the SABUA for their decision. The question, in view of Jones's umpiring experience at other levels of competition, is whether this is a valid defense. Judge Thompson did not address this issue in his opinion because the SABUA's motion for summary judgment raised only the issue of whether it was covered at all under the ADA.

A recent issue that has arisen under the ADA is whether officiating is a major life activity and thus whether the inability to officiate is proof of a disability. The U.S. District Court for the Northern District of Illinois in 1997 dismissed football official Lorenzo Clemons's lawsuit against the Big Ten Conference. Clemons filed the lawsuit in January 1995, claiming that he was terminated after six seasons because the supervisor of football officials, David Parry, perceived that Clemons was disabled because Clemons weighed 285 pounds. This court found that being denied the opportunity to referee college football is not a substantial limitation of a major life activity.

From 1988 through 1993, Clemons officiated approximately 11 games a year. When hired by the conference, Clemons weighed 235 pounds, but he continued to gain weight. In 1990, Parry implemented a rating system for his football officials comprising evaluations by the game coaches, observers who were former football officials, and Parry. In the first year of the evaluation system, Clemons rated 36th out of 44 officials. In 1991, he was rated 49th out of 49 officials. At the conclusion of both seasons, Parry discussed Clemons's weight with him and its effect on his performance.

In 1993, Clemons was rated 43rd out of 45 officials, and his written evaluation pointed out that his weight—277 pounds at the beginning of the 1993 season and 280 at its conclusion—affected his performance. During the season he had made 12 errors in judgment, the most of any conference official. Parry told Clemons to lose 10 pounds and placed him on probation. Clemons reported to the pre-1994 season clinic at 285 pounds, whereupon his contract for the 1994 season was terminated. Clemons continued his regular full-time job as Inter-Governmental Liaison for the Cook County (Illinois) Sheriff's Office. Clemons and the conference agreed that his weight had no effect on that job.

The court agreed with the legal arguments made by the Big Ten Conference that the conference had not perceived him as disabled—possessing an impairment that substantially limited the major life activities of work—as defined by the ADA. To satisfy this burden of proof, Clemons was required to show under the ADA that (1) he suffers from a disability as defined in the ADA; (2) he is otherwise qualified to perform his job; and (3) he was discharged because of his disability. To prevail on his claim he had to show that he had an impairment that substantially limited a major life activity. One such major life activity under the ADA is working. However, as defined by the law, the inability to perform a single, particular job does not constitute a substantial limitation on working. The regulations interpreting the ADA note that "except in rare circumstances, obesity is not considered a disabling impairment."

District Judge William T. Hart determined that Clemons could not have been perceived to be disabled because he was not permitted to work as a referee only for 11 days, and he could and did work at his regular job. The court determined that he was not substantially limited in the major life activity of working and dismissed his claim.

This decision, if followed by other courts, means that at least football officials, and perhaps all nonprofessional officials, will not be able to use inability to officiate as proof of a disability under the ADA. Officiating, because it is often an avocation, may not be within the ADA's definition of a major life activity. An official may, however, still be able to succeed on such a claim under certain states' laws against discrimination that do not have such definitional limitations.

Sports Officials' Associations

More than 4,000 local sports officials' associations operate in the United States. As officiating has

grown as a profession, so too has the manner in which sports officials' associations conduct their business. Many of these groups are voluntary nonprofit membership organizations, while others are profit-making businesses operated by one or more people. Both types train and assign their officials to games.

Business Structure

Most officials' associations operate as profit corporations, sole proprietorships, unincorporated associations, or nonprofit corporations. For voluntary membership groups, the best form of business is a nonprofit corporation organized for educational purposes. This is easily accomplished by filing articles or a certificate of incorporation with the state and is relatively inexpensive. The filing fees and attorneys' fees are approximately $500 to $1,000, depending on the state. This is not expensive when compared with the liability of individual members should the association be sued.

The most important reason for incorporation is to protect the association officers and members from liability for contractual or injury claims. If an association incorporates, only the corporation, not the officials involved in the corporation, has potential liability. For example, what happens if a member is authorized by an association to buy jackets for all officials but fails to pay for them? If the local association is unincorporated, every member would be individually liable for the full amount due. If the association is a corporation, however, only the corporation, and therefore the corporate treasury, is required to pay the debt if the store sues and obtains a judgment.

Similarly, if a member is sued by a player who claims that she was injured by the official's negligence, the association will likely be joined in the lawsuit as a defendant. The claim will be that the association failed to train the official properly. If the association is not a corporation, each official and officer may be responsible to pay any judgment, legal fees, and costs awarded to the player.

The Russ Fendley Sports Officials' Association in California discovered this problem. It was an unincorporated association of umpires. One of its members was sued by the City of Long

Beach, which had been sued by a player in a recreational baseball game whose leg was injured by the base spike when sliding into second base. Each member of the group had potential liability for the judgment rendered for the player.

Corporate Bylaws

In conjunction with incorporation, an officials' association should also adopt bylaws, the operating rules of the group. One of the most unpleasant tasks sports officials' groups must occasionally perform is disciplining their members. If disciplinary procedure is not well planned or not performed properly, it may create serious legal problems for a local association.

An Ohio wrongful expulsion lawsuit brought by an umpire against his association focused attention on how officials' groups may discipline their members. In that case, the umpire alleged that he was expelled from membership for bad-faith reasons and in violation of his constitutional, procedural due-process rights by not being given an appropriate hearing. The judge dismissed the suit, ruling that the association acted properly and within the scope of its constitution.

Losing such a case can be avoided by providing appropriate provisions in the bylaws. Unacceptable behavior should be clearly defined so that members are aware of required and prohibited activities. For example, violations of a game-assigning system, specific conduct unbecoming an official, the requirement of taking and passing an annual written rules test, and meeting attendance requirements should be specified. Each member should be given a copy of the bylaws.

In addition to listing required and prohibited activities, the bylaws should also include the procedure for handling violations. The penalties that might be imposed, such as fines, suspension, or expulsion, for various violations should be included in the bylaws. The key elements to keep in mind in drafting these due-process provisions are that they must provide the member reasonable notice of the alleged violation, a reasonable opportunity to present his or her side of the story, reasonable notice of the possible penalty, and a right to appeal.

Notice of a violation should be given to a member in writing by certified mail, return receipt requested. The notice should include a brief explanation of the alleged violation, the date of the violation, the names of the people who filed the allegation, the possible penalty, and a reference to the bylaw provision that provides the procedure for the member to be heard and to present his or her version of the incident.

The member must then be given the opportunity to present his or her account by appearing with any witnesses and documentary evidence to support his or her side before the appropriate committee for the group. The proceeding should begin with the presentation of the charge, the possible penalty, and evidence against the member. People who have knowledge about the incident should also tell their stories. All this should be done with the accused member present so that he or she may ask questions if desired. The accused member then should be permitted to present his or her side with witnesses and documents. The committee should make its decision, including any penalty, and communicate it in writing to the member by certified mail, return receipt requested.

The member should have an opportunity to appeal an adverse decision. The bylaws should include a provision that a member may appeal to the executive board by requesting an appeal within a certain number of days after the decision has been rendered. The executive board can then schedule a meeting to consider the appeal or can decide to hold another full hearing. The decision of the executive board should also be communicated in writing to the member.

The group should also keep and retain accurate records of all proceedings concerning the disciplining of members. The group should keep copies of all letters sent and received and minutes of all general membership meetings and executive board meetings so that a complete record will be available if needed. An officer should retain these records in a specific location and pass them on when there is a change of administration. It is not unusual for a lawsuit to be filed a year or more after the relevant events took place.

The key to bylaws is that they be reasonable and fair. Courts have generally upheld provisions if those prerequisites are followed. Bylaws not only protect an association from future legal problems in the disciplining of members, but also help a group to function in an even-handed manner.

Sample Bylaws

The following sections provide sample text of corporate bylaws for an officials' association.

Examinations

Every active member shall take the written examination as cadets take. Such examination shall be issued to every active member at the first board meeting following the date of the cadet test. Any member who fails to attain a passing grade must attend a special meeting to be held by the rules interpreter.

Meetings

Section 1. Number. There shall be a minimum of seven (7) meetings between October and April of each year.

Section 2. Notice. Notices shall be sent out by the secretary-treasurer prior to October of each year.

Section 3. Attendance. Active members including dual members must attend at least four (4) meetings between October and April of each year, one of which must be a rules interpretation meeting.

Conduct

All members shall conduct themselves at all times while engaged in officiating duties and officiating-related duties in a manner becoming to an official.

Discipline of Members

Section 1. Grounds for discipline. For failure to comply with established authority or regulation of the board; delinquency in payment of authorized charges, fines, penalties, or assessments; or for any other conduct conclusively established to be contrary to the best interest of basketball, a member may be placed on probation or suspended from the board for not more than one year or may be expelled through the actions of the executive committee.

Section 2. Appeal. Any member suspended by the board shall have the right of appeal to the executive committee.

Section 3. Right of Hearing. A member charged with any violation shall have the right to be heard in person or by written statement made by the member in his or her own defense. Such right shall be afforded prior to the imposition of any fine, penalty, or any other disciplinary action, and thereupon a member may seek a personal hearing if the member makes a request in writing to the member who sent the notification of a violation within fourteen (14) days of the date of the notification. A member may then appeal the determination to the executive committee by giving the executive committee written notice within seven (7) days of the receipt of the determination. The executive committee may then decide the matter on the facts and determination previously made or by asking the member to personally appear.

Section 4. Discipline Notice. When a member is suspended or expelled, the executive committee shall notify all concerned that such a member is no longer able to accept assignments or officiate as a member of this board. No active member shall officiate knowingly with a suspended or expelled member.

Insurance

It is important for local officials' associations, as well as all individual members, to have liability insurance. This insurance pays attorneys' fees and costs should the association or its members be sued for negligence, defamation, civil rights violations, or other types of related claims. Two types of policies must be purchased: one for the association and the other by each member individually. Both types of policies are available from several sources, including NASO. An association should also have a directors' and officers' liability policy to cover it for claims regarding decisions and official policies of the association and its committees.

Contracts

Officials' associations should, as a good business practice, prepare and require each member official and hiring school to complete a written contract for each game. Such a contract helps avoid misunderstandings and lawsuits. Several provisions are important to include: game date and place, official's legal status, payment, and what happens if the game is cancelled or postponed.

Summary

The keys to avoiding legal problems for officials and officials' associations are awareness of potential liability claims and good business practices. As Ralph Waldo Emerson said: "Knowledge is the antidote to fear." Knowledge, it is hoped, will reduce player injuries and poorly reasoned decisions by officials and their associations, thereby resulting in fewer claims against officials. A strong educational commitment is essential in today's economic, business, and legal sports environment.

Officials may not be aware of how they themselves are protected when they step on a floor or field to work a contest. This chapter provided several cases that illustrate how laws protect officials' civil rights. Officiating associations should also take steps to ensure fairness as they strive to serve both schools and member officials. Because sports officiating requires additional commitments from individuals, the next chapter demonstrates ways to organize time effectively.

11

Time Management

Jerry Grunska

In this chapter you'll learn

- the importance of managing time well,

- causes of poor time management,

- how to evaluate your time-management skills, and

- how to improve your time management.

Anytime you add an activity to your life, you must make accommodations for it. Finding the time needed to perform competently as an official takes a special kind of planning. Sports officiating often necessitates covering games in the evening and on weekends, times that many people usually consider "free." This chapter shows the types of time commitments necessary to succeed as an official, illustrates the problems of arranging for that time, and offers advice about how to meet your time commitments.

Officials as Time Managers

If your life is busy, a commitment to officiating requires your wedging in blocks of time to ensure that your sports enterprise will be of a high caliber. If you take a casual approach, showing only partial dedication to becoming a top-flight performer, you are not likely to rise above mediocrity.

Because you no doubt need to accommodate the requirements of officiating along with those of your primary career and other obligations, such as family commitments, time is a precious commodity that should not be wasted. It is vital to understand seven types of additional time commitments that officials must make. None of these time requirements can be overlooked.

1. *Time for games.* Contests usually last from one to three hours, depending on the sport, and often you'll be asked to officiate several games in succession, particularly at the high school underclass level. Schools ordinarily schedule varsity games on Friday nights and Saturdays, but some varsity sports and many underclass programs can take place any weekday, usually after school around 4:00 P.M.

2. *Time for travel.* If you live an hour away from a game site, plan for three hours of travel time: two hours there and back, plus an extra half hour before and after the game.

3. *Time for on-site game preparation.* In many sports, officials wear a special uniform and are expected to be at a site in time to change and even to warm up. Also, many sports require the official to conduct pregame inspections such as checking score books and equipment. Some rule books insist that officials observe player warm-ups a half hour before the start of games.

4. *Time for on-site mental preparation.* Several sports require pregame conferences for officials, so that they can exchange ideas about preferred techniques, agree on crew synchrony, and review key rules to prepare for the upcoming contest. If the crew travels together, this orienting can take place on the way to the game, but sometimes this opportunity is not available.

5. *Time for book learning.* The rules of each sport and their myriad applications are intricate, difficult to digest, and they require study. Some sources recommend reading a single rule at a time or spending 15 to 20 minutes a day in diligent perusal. Often a good way to solidify learning is to discuss ramifications of rules with fellow officials or to participate in formal class discussions.

6. *Time for practical learning.* Few officials feel comfortable going into a season "cold," so they customarily attend clinics in the off-season for simulations, walk-through experiences, and game tips. Also, school coaches frequently ask officials to handle preseason scrimmages, which are excellent opportunities for officials to review and practice their skills before the season.

7. *Time for meetings.* Officials' associations are charged with the task of introducing new rules and upgrading officiating knowledge. Not all local groups are organized to perform these tasks, serving instead as social gatherings and assigning forums, but a fortunate number of associations strive to fulfill a training function. Often, officiating groups meet several times before the season and weekly thereafter.

Making Time for Officiating

The following examples illustrate the importance of patience, compromise, and creativity in time management.

• Delrose Hoile of Breckenridge, Minnesota, mother of three preteens, found herself having to cancel some enjoyable activities and alter others in order to undertake an officiating commitment. Her specialties were volleyball and softball, sports she had played in high school.

Officiating meetings were on Wednesday nights, which was her church choir rehearsal night. Reluctantly, she decided to give up singing, though she made it a point to listen to the choir in church on Sundays. Games were on nights when she customarily supervised her youngsters' homework sessions. She asked her husband to forgo watching Monday night football on television and oversee the children's study time instead. (He still managed to view the second half!) Delrose also stopped going to a Thursday noon kaffeeklatsch with three neighbors during the season, setting that time aside as "rule book time." To keep posted on community news, she arranged each day to stop at one neighbor's house when walking the dog.

• Ron Wright of Williston, North Dakota, had to choose between scuba diving and officiating basketball games. As long as he worked junior high and junior varsity games, he was able to stop at the local YMCA for diving lessons on Friday evenings. Promotion to varsity games obliged Wright to drop his enjoyable aquatic hobby. But the promotion had a plus side, too. He put aside his varsity earnings and indulged in a diving expedition to the Dry Tortugas after the season.

Common Errors in Managing Time

Selectivity and careful planning are key words in managing time. *Squandering* is the opposite of making conscious choices. No one likes to have vital plans interrupted or derailed. Specific steps for making sure time is carefully allocated are explained later, but first we identify some common pitfalls.

Certain habits and behaviors can cause a person literally to lose time and can deprive an official of valuable opportunities. This doesn't mean that you must have your nose to the grindstone continually or give up leisure pleasures entirely, but it does mean thinking positively about using time well and establishing priorities. See if any of the following habits relate to problems you have:

1. *Relying on "mythical time" to fulfill obligations.* Some people permit a task to draw out, believing that they can finish later, when in fact the time left for completion diminishes. You might be less efficient than you presume, be thrown off schedule by interruptions, or improperly estimate the time needed for preliminary tasks. Therefore, anticipated time is an illusion that fades away, resulting in a project that may be hurried, poorly finished, or incomplete due to calculating the time requirements inaccurately. An official may intend to study the rules on a regular basis, for example, but the time never comes, so the individual starts the season with gaps in preparation.

2. *Putting things off.* Often the least appealing responsibility is pushed aside, then the time needed to work on the task disappears. For example, an official may vow to notify the assignor of availability but misses the deadline and therefore is deprived of a decent game schedule.

3. *Being unaware of "task hopping."* Failure to complete one task before undertaking another means that a person is a "juggler" who tries to keep too many things going at once and does not do a thorough job with any of them. People guilty of this practice fail to meet deadlines and end up doing a shoddy job because they are behind, and

their mistakes are often costly. Some officials work so many games, sometimes even shifting from one sport to another on a given day, that they become officiating vagabonds, hurrying from venue to venue in perpetual motion. It is impossible for them to be good at what they are attempting.

4. *Faulty concentration.* In their primary occupations, people with poor concentration may procrastinate or be sidetracked by distractions such as doodling, a trip to the water cooler, or chatting with colleagues. The inability to zero in on necessary tasks is caused by a failure to prioritize and results in a lack of follow-through, that is, not finishing what you start. Though a lack of concentration during a game can cause the quality of

The time actually spent working games will be but a small percentage of the time needed to do justice to yourself and the sport and to achieve excellence.

Out of Control

Gregory Samsar, a Bluffton, Ohio, volleyball official, was asked by a neighborhood group to serve on a community caucus for local elections. He was also asked to serve on the entertainment committee for a PTA fun fair. Both groups scheduled sessions for a Tuesday evening, and Samsar found that his Tuesday afternoon volleyball assignment spilled over into the caucus meeting.

He arrived late at the caucus meeting and was greeted with amused expressions because he still had his uniform on. "We'll make you jail keeper," one member said, and another suggested that Samsar might make a good animal control committee chairman. Samsar had to excuse himself to make the PTA meeting, where he was again late and subtly ridiculed.

Before long, he found himself recommended for the balloon toss at the PTA fun fair. He'd wear his officiating uniform, and children would pay several cents to bombard him for prizes. "Everybody likes to pick on referees," the nominating individual said. Nonplussed, Samsar acquiesced in this dubious appointment.

When Samsar arrived home that evening, he found a phone message that said he'd been named chairman of the animal control committee. "Never again," he told his wife, who was sympathetic but aware of his reluctance to say no. "First I'll have to corral mad dogs and then be a living target for wild-eyed kids. I'm going to think twice before I volunteer again."

The reality of "dead time" tends to prolong games beyond ordinary expectations. Each sport requires a distinct signal for indicating that play has stopped. In baseball and softball a vigorous thrust upward of both arms says that a hit has been declared foul or that another player act has resulted in live action being temporarily halted.

your officiating to suffer, it also creates problems before and after games because it prevents you from making the most efficient use of your time.

5. *Ignoring reality.* Some people don't know when they've overloaded themselves and have made too many commitments. Taking on an extra chore may indicate that you're willing to extend yourself, but you may not have time to meet that additional obligation.

Evaluating Your Time Management Skills

Estimate your effectiveness in managing time by completing the self-evaluation questionnaire on the next page. Circle your answers or jot them on a separate sheet of paper and add them up for your total.

If you have been honest with yourself, you can tell by the items you marked which areas need improvement. If you scored worse than you would like, consult the following guidelines for improving your time management skills.

Improving Your Time Management Skills

You can always improve the way you manage your time. Even if you're satisfied with your efficiency level, take a look at the list that follows. It will help you organize your tasks without feeling overwhelmed by them.

▮ Set aside time for planning your tasks. Isolate yourself, if possible, to concentrate on step-by-step approaches to getting things done. Planning will save time in the long run, as it gives you a chance to prioritize your tasks before you begin them.

▮ Define your goals on paper, preferably each week, so that they can be reviewed daily and checked off when they are reached. Writing down your weekly goals gives you a chance to see and evaluate what you plan to accomplish. Break down weekly goals into daily goals to make them more manageable.

Time necessary for games is easy to underestimate, what with unanticipated extra innings and overtimes. Managing time effectively means taking into account the possible expansion of commitments.

Time Management Self-Assessment

1. To what extent do I plan my time?

1	2	3	4	5
always	frequently	sometimes	seldom	never

2. To what extent do I set and stick to priorities?

1	2	3	4	5
always	frequently	sometimes	seldom	never

3. To what extent do I waste time on such things as chatter, indulgences, and diversions?

1	2	3	4	5
never	seldom	sometimes	frequently	always

4. To what extent do I permit telephone interruptions?

1	2	3	4	5
never	seldom	sometimes	frequently	always

5. To what extent do I waste time in meetings (by my own choice)?

1	2	3	4	5
never	seldom	sometimes	frequently	always

6. To what extent do I lose time due to inefficient paperwork processing?

1	2	3	4	5
never	seldom	sometimes	frequently	always

7. To what extent do I overcommit to obligations?

1	2	3	4	5
never	seldom	sometimes	frequently	always

8. To what extent do I procrastinate and avoid immersing myself in a task?

1	2	3	4	5
never	seldom	sometimes	frequently	always

9. To what extent do I delegate work and share responsibilities?

1	2	3	4	5
always	frequently	sometimes	seldom	never

10. To what extent do I engage in "task hopping," leaving projects unfinished?

1	2	3	4	5
never	seldom	sometimes	frequently	always

Total your score and compare it with the scale below.

Range	Rating
10–15	Outstanding
16–20	Superior
21–25	Good
26–30	Mediocre
31–50	Weak

■ Establish tentative time frames for task completion. Having done a specific task before will help you determine realistic guidelines. Simply having a time estimate will also make you more conscious of how you spend your time and thus more likely to spend it efficiently.

■ Identify onerous tasks and place them in the priority list. Be sure to earmark responsibilities that require immediate attention.

■ Establish a routine; do not dilute or neglect everyday duties.

■ Adhere to deadlines, and monitor your success in this regard. Reward yourself for meeting your goals.

■ Delegate whenever possible, and do not let your ego stand in the way of turning over responsibility and praising individuals for their accomplishments.

■ Don't let others waste your time, and don't waste colleagues' time. Practice terminating conversations gently but firmly in person and over the phone.

■ Learn to make rapid and smooth transitions between tasks, and monitor your own progress in this endeavor.

■ Monitor the degree of stress you are experiencing in completing tasks. Strive to be upbeat about digging into challenges. Talk yourself into being a happy worker. State of mind is largely a chosen attitude.

■ When others place burdens on you or when tasks seem overwhelming, take a mental break and reestablish your goals. Make sure that your original goals are flexible enough to deal with unforeseen circumstances. Try not to let surprises upset you.

■ Try to erase from your mind the responsibilities of work when you are away from it, and seize time for enjoyment. Make a private vow that you will not feel guilty for maintaining your emotional stability.

Summary

If people took stock of how their time is spent on a given day, many of them would be surprised at how many interruptions they are forced to deal with. For example, few people plan for intrusions via telephone. The time spent on personal chats would also be startling for many people.

This chapter showed seven necessary time commitments in officiating. If you find yourself continually pressed for time, examine the probable causes of faulty time management. The self-assessment tool in this chapter can show you the personal habits you may need to change in order to make effective use of time. We also offered ways to make those changes.

The next part of this book highlights sports officiating as a career, starting with an examination of officiating associations.

Part V
....
The Officiating
Profession

12

Working With Associations

Henry Zaborniak, Jr.

In this chapter you'll learn

- six benefits of working with local officiating associations,

- what a regional or local association can offer,

- the hierarchy of associations that serve high school sports officials, and

- how associations serve both the sports enterprise and officials.

The process of becoming a high school sports official involves registering with the state high school organization that handles accreditation. Most schools cannot employ you unless you are formally affiliated with the state office that governs interscholastic sports. Usually that means passing one or more tests to obtain approval. Such tests assess your knowledge of the rules and mechanics of your sport. State organizations, as well as regional and national ones, are mostly concerned with rules and policies for various sports.

Working With Local Officiating Organizations

In addition to registering with the state, you can benefit considerably by participating in a local officials' group. Each large city in the country has at least one officials' association, and many smaller towns do also. Their functions vary, but often local associations are responsible for training officials and assigning them to games.

Local organizations usually dedicate themselves to improving officiating and to serving schools, recreation departments, and private sports clubs. (Popular sports such as hockey and soccer are sometimes sponsored by private organizations.) An official can benefit by attending the meetings of a local association; in some locales, belonging to a local association is mandatory. These groups generally meet regularly—sometimes weekly—before and during the sports season. You can benefit from these organizations in many ways:

■ *Sharing experience.* A local association can offer a connection with like-minded individuals, people who already are or intend to be sports officials. By mingling with others who officiate, you can further develop skills as an official, as well as help those with less experience than you through shop talk and shared experiences.

■ *Getting support.* A local association can offer a foundation of support for its members. It is sometimes necessary for an intermediary to help solve problems that arise during games or that involve stipends and game conditions. For example, some associations insist that officials have escorts to and from locker rooms, that a game administrator be available for all contests, and that payment for games takes place as the officials are dressing for the contest. Associations are in a position to act on behalf of members, securing privileges and rights, where an individual might have a slender chance of affecting policy. If particular coaches, schools, or leagues mistreat officials in

some way—by making them dress in unpleasant cubbyholes, for example, or permitting spectators access to officials' quarters—an association is more likely to effect a change in such practices than a single official who registers an objection.

■ *Learning more about officiating.* More and more officials are asking for help in learning sophisticated approaches to working games. Sometimes this help can come from outside sources, such as clinics held by independent organizations or classes conducted in community colleges, but often local associations take it upon themselves to establish formal orientation sessions for beginners and advanced instructional programs for veteran officials.

It is important to note that not all associations have full-fledged programs to assist officials in learning and improving. The quality of instruction varies a great deal from one group to another.

■ *Getting more games.* Officiating associations often are primarily responsible for assigning officials to games. Again, the degree of involvement with leagues and schools varies from region to region, but many associations consider appointments to be their primary function. This means that officials who operate independently, without joining an association, are by and large left out of the assigning process. Belonging to an association is often requisite for getting game assignments.

An Effective Mentoring System

An officiating association in Rockford, Illinois, headed by Gary Gullett, has developed a workable mentoring system that engages experienced officials in the orienting of new members. Rookies draw up a brief résumé of their experience, including the college they attended, their hobbies, and how they want to be perceived as officials, then volunteer mentors select the individuals that they want to tutor based on their résumés. First, the mentors are instructed in ways to help newcomers, which include writing up a review of a beginner in action. The review must include four positive statements for every negative one so that the beginners are not overwhelmed by criticism. The mentors are also advised to look for fundamentals in game coverage by beginners and not to expect sophisticated behavior. Mentors must observe rookies twice in game situations, and rookies in turn must see their mentors perform twice. Both are encouraged to chat between observations and to sit in on pregame conferences and postgame wrap-ups. The mentors have to submit a final report to the association's education committee at season's end to verify completion of their commitment. The new officials are also asked to describe how they felt about the mentoring experience.

Staying informed. Associations often establish policies and procedures for their members that may extend beyond the guidelines of officiating manuals. For instance, an association may require its members to wear special patches on their uniforms, it may specify the steps to take at a game site in preparing for a game, and it may insist that members follow certain guidelines when talking to players or coaches during games. Such policies outline tactics that are not dealt with in officiating manuals or formal publications. Another benefit of belonging to an association is learning local and regional practices, including how to handle situations that aren't covered by the manual.

Being social. Participating in a local association's activities is a good way to meet like-minded individuals and make friends. Bonding with people who share a common interest is a special feature of belonging to a formal officials' group, because people who officiate sports often share numerous experiences that are very satisfying, as well as occasional trying times when a crew was hard-pressed to solve a problem. By undergoing a periodic "trial by fire," officials develop a kinship that may go beyond mere camaraderie. Officials who stay dedicated to their sport often find that their firmest friendships are with other officials.

Local associations often have celebrations too, such as season-ending banquets and recreational outings. These social engagements serve to join people together in harmony. It is wise to keep in mind that often an official's only support in a hotly contested game is a fellow official.

Serving your community. Some local or regional associations serve another vital civic function, namely, providing support for the community. Like other service clubs such as Rotary or Kiwanis, they volunteer at nursing homes and soup kitchens for the homeless, contribute to charities, and gather gifts for underprivileged youngsters. You might derive a great deal of satisfaction from partaking in such activities or from serving the association as a recruiter, policy committee representative, or recording secretary. Volunteerism has its own rewards.

© Referee

Along with an in-depth written review, a meeting between a rookie official and his or her mentors immediately following a contest, while specific events are still fresh in mind, can only benefit the newcomer.

A Good Cause

An officials' association in Mundelein, Illinois, has established a scholarship endowment at a nearby high school in Buffalo Grove. The scholarship is in memory of a long-time association leader, Norman Geske. Funds have been raised through raffles, fun fairs, and contributions. Every season, officials in that group pledge one game fee for the fund. Each year, the athletic department at Buffalo Grove selects as a recipient one senior who has been a strong scholar and a contributing athlete but is unlikely to be offered a college athletic scholarship. Scholarships have been awarded for over a dozen years.

How Local Associations Train Members

A beginning official should expect the local officials' association to offer education in how rules are applied in game situations and in preferred types of mechanics. Such education is best done in a formal setting, with demonstrations, films, explanations, and walk-through simulations. Instruction should be offered to experienced officials to upgrade their knowledge as well as to new officials to introduce intricate aspects of game management.

An ideal educational system uses systematic planning to develop a viable curriculum for training officials. The intensity and thoroughness of such training systems vary from one group to another. One association may have a carefully developed instructional program that is offered year after year, whereas another association in the same community may operate haphazardly, with little useful instruction at all. No national training curriculum or standardized instruction has been developed for officials. Soccer officials have the most comprehensive program in place, but this program was devised by an outside source, not by a national interscholastic sports group.

In addition to learning the fundamentals of how to observe play during games, to work effectively with partners, and to interpret the rules, officials should expect a local association to help with such things as making proper judgments and working diplomatically with coaches and players. These two areas are critical in an official's development. Ultimately, whether or not an official succeeds in officiating depends on the way that official judges play action: meting out penalties, bypassing borderline infractions, and making calls consistently. An umpire with a faulty strike zone is unlikely to succeed until such a deficiency is corrected.

How Local Organizations Assign Games

Some local associations exist primarily to place officials at game sites, though the degree of associations' involvement in game assignments varies from region to region. In some places, conferences and leagues may turn over their entire sports schedules, including all levels of a given sport, to an officiating association, or they may split the assignments between several groups to promote fairness. On the other hand, some associations have only minimal involvement in assigning officials. That responsibility may lie with an appointed individual who has no connection to any officials' association; it may be a school administrator or an outside assigning authority.

When an association has a strong voice in who gets what games, the issue of fair distribution is often contentious. A new official should discover the protocols for obtaining game assignments, both the formal elements and the accepted procedures for establishing relationships with people in control of assigning games. People who assign games, for instance, need to know who you are, your qualifications, when you are available to work, and your level of expertise.

Most often the way to make the acquaintance of an assigning authority is to produce a résumé, citing your age, experience, occupation, and instructional background (whether or not you've had formal training in officiating). You can sometimes also rely on personal networking within your association. It is important not to exagger-

© Bob Messina

Ultimately, success in officiating depends on the way an official judges play action and manages participants.

ate anything about your past officiating experience. Officials who try to work beyond their capacity are likely to be exposed by their shortcomings and hence reduce their chances of becoming regular practitioners.

Many assignors are elected by local associations. Sometimes assignors act independently, but in some instances leagues and coaches evaluate and recommend the officials who will handle their games. The ultimate purpose of a competent assignor is to match games with the best officials possible, considering officials' experience, place of residence (so as to avoid potential conflicts), and reputation. Some associations have policies about where an official can work, how much experience is essential before varsity assignments are made, how many games can be worked in a particular league, and so on. Trying to buck the system because you are dissatisfied with it is seldom successful and can give you a bad reputation as a renegade.

In many places, soliciting games—either by contacting schools or by personal appeals to as-

signors—is not permitted. You must learn the avenues of entry and advancement for the given locale. Being overly aggressive in trying to establish yourself is usually looked on as a breach of decorum. You must discover a careful, diplomatic balance in deportment when entering officiating circles.

State High School Associations

Every state in the United States has an organization that oversees interscholastic high school athletics. (See Appendix B for names and addresses of respective state associations.) Though these associations differ in the scope of their duties, their basic purpose is to govern the way sports are played between schools. These organizations set player eligibility guidelines, the number of contests allowed per sport per season, practice times and dates, and other policies that all mem-

A new official should discover the protocols for obtaining assignments. Those who assign contests need to know who you are, your qualifications, when you are available to work, and your level of expertise.

offs such as baseball, softball, volleyball, basketball, and football. Such clinics are usually held on a weekend; there may be regional clinics or one statewide clinic at a central location. Often attendance is necessary for officials to be considered for play-off assignments. The clinics are an effort to standardize officiating techniques throughout the state and to upgrade officials' knowledge on a statewide scale by acquainting them with up-to-date officiating techniques. State associations ordinarily rely on experienced officials within the state as clinic instructors.

State associations establish regulations for officials, such as how many association meetings an official must attend, the yearly requirements that must be met for continued certification, and the category in which an official is listed. Some states designate levels of expertise, and officials must meet certain criteria to move from one level to the next. Often this is a matter of passing a test with a high grade, favorable coaches' ratings, and a specified amount of experience. Some state associations appoint rule interpreters who deliver information about new rules and changes that the state has made in matters of competition to all officials in the state before a sport season. This is one way that an official can interact with representatives of the state governing body.

ber schools must obey. Some state associations extend their influence to include such things as band and orchestra competition, cheerleading clinics, and drama and debate competitions.

State associations generally handle registration of sports officials, which means that a person must pay a fee and take tests to be allowed to officiate in that state. A few states delegate this task to local associations. Some states also provide officials with excess medical insurance, liability insurance, and fee-loss insurance. Addresses and phone numbers of local associations are often available from state organizations; some states produce a directory of local groups.

State associations depend on local associations to recruit and train officials. The state associations generally leave the details of educating officials up to local associations, although about half the states sponsor officiating clinics in various sports, especially those that lead to state play-

The National Federation of State High School Associations

The governing body for all 50 states' interscholastic high school athletics, the National Federation of State High School Associations, is an arm of the state associations. Policies are determined by representatives from various states, and mandates are administered by a top administrator and staff. This organization makes rule changes, certifies coaches through special training sessions, and produces the rule books and officiating manuals for every sport. Officials can purchase these publications as well as uniforms from the Federation. The Federation serves the schools primarily, but it also enforces policies that affect officials. The officiating uniform for each sport is

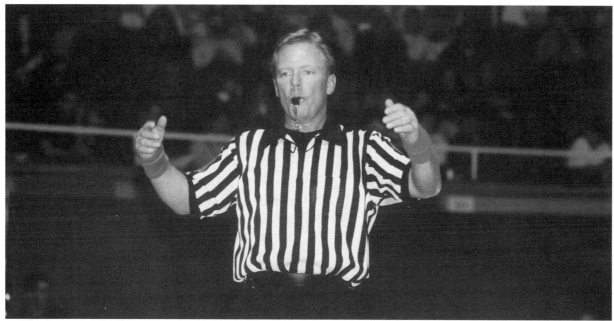

Often, officials must attend statewide or regional clinics in order to be considered for high school play-off assignments.

determined by the Federation, though individual states are free to make some modifications. Jackets, gloves, whether officials can have advertising slogans on their apparel, and so forth are other uniform details that are left to the states' discretion.

The Federation also has a far-reaching program of insurance to protect officials. In most, though not all, states, an official who registers with that state is also registered with the national federation and is covered by a blanket insurance policy for injuries sustained during play and for liability issues arising from game circumstances.

Defining NASO and its Operation

The National Association of Sports Officials (NASO; see Appendix C) is the leading sports officials' group in the United States with a membership of more than 20,000 individuals who officiate athletic contests from youth through professional levels.

The functions of this 25-year-old organization are broad in scope, ranging from insurance coverage to educational services. It is the nation's primary advocate on behalf of sports officials, in all sports and across all levels. It has sent representatives to various forums for promoting sportsmanship. It has advised state legislatures on preparing bills that provide punishment for people who assault officials. It has worked with state associations to upgrade instructional programs. For more than a dozen years it has sponsored national conventions where exchanges of viewpoints take place.

Its affiliate, Referee Enterprises, Inc., publishes a monthly magazine, *Referee*, with ongoing advisories about working games in prominent sports. The magazine also contains officiating news from around the country and feature articles that probe areas of interest to sports officials.

This latter organization also produces books for sports officials and provides information about organizational policies for local associations, about legal issues, and about business practices. It has provided the major impetus for development of this book.

NASO's bylaws include the following stipulations about its overall purpose:

1. To provide education programs to advance the professional skills of sports officials at all levels of competition.

2. To conduct studies and analyses of athletic contest rules to identify sources of officiating problems and to seek solutions in cooperation with appropriate rules-making bodies.

3. To place special emphasis on developing concepts of good sportsmanship.

4. To advance respect for authority of officials at all levels of competition.

Summary

To work high school games, an official must be affiliated with the state scholastic governing body. In some states, that means membership in a local association, and in most if not all states that means paying a fee, purchasing rule books, and registering with the state office that governs interscholastic athletics.

The state and national organizations make the rules for various sports and determine game policies. Local associations can serve officials in many ways, such as insisting on protection at games and appealing for increases in stipends.

Local organizations are frequently responsible for recruiting, training, and assigning officials. Leagues and state associations customarily leave those tasks up to regional officiating groups, although state associations themselves usually appoint officials to state tournaments. Local organizations also determine some aspects of how games are handled in their vicinity.

Becoming an accredited high school official is only the first step in your profession. The next chapter explains how officiating sports can become a long-term, even a lifetime, career.

13

Officiating: A Lifetime Career

Henry Zaborniak, Jr.

In this chapter you'll learn

- ways to improve your officiating skills,

- how to advance from one level to another, and

- ways to derive continued satisfaction from officiating.

Sports officiating can be a lifetime career, but the type of career you build is up to you. Some officials prefer to operate at a low-key level, maybe even forgoing the opportunity to work high school varsity sports. Officiating is strictly a recreational experience for them, and their enjoyment rests in serving others in a useful capacity. Others are pleased when they attain varsity status and are content to work diligently in that realm. Still oth-ers seek to move up to more demanding levels: college or even professional sports.

Whatever level officials wish to aim for, they can enjoy the experience for a long time if they continue to improve. Former NFL referee Jerry Markbreit said, "The perfect game hasn't been worked yet, but that's no reason to stop trying." Ongoing study of rules and techniques is one way to continue growing. If officials cease trying to get better, from lack of motivation or limitations in ability, they stagnate and may just go through the motions when working games.

Officials who aspire to higher levels must learn accepted procedures for advancing, which differ from region to region. Camps and clinics are of-ten opportunities for advancement. Information about regional and national camps, clinics, and conventions can be obtained from the National Association of Sports Officials (see Appendix C). Strong networking, which may include seeking a mentor, can help foster advancement. Improve-ment also comes from honest self-assessment and

For many officials, officiating is primarily a recreational experience, where the main enjoyment rests in serving others. Here, umpire Harvey Everette helps his grandson Lashawn run the bases during a T-ball game.

from modeling the behavior of established officials.

To feel good about an extended career, officials should have nearly as much fun working a game as participants have playing. Though officials usually have to work more than play, those who make officiating a lifetime career find their work satisfying and enjoyable.

Improving Skills

As in many other fields of endeavor, it is possible to work toward a certain goal in officiating—for instance, obtaining a satisfactory high school varsity schedule—and then fall into the habit of taking your skills for granted and not seeking to improve. Officials have a tendency to be self-satisfied once they reach a certain level of expertise. They often don't take constructive criticism well, nor do they seek evaluation from experts. In fact, they may not acknowledge that anyone could critique their work fairly, and they close their minds to the prospect of altering their habits. Faulty habits sometimes hold officials back at one level, preventing them from improving and advancing. The gratification of a full schedule is one factor that stifles improvement, but other factors operate as well. You will seldom get a critical review from an objective source that identifies your strengths and weaknesses. Also, you will seldom have opportunities to witness techniques that are more advanced than your own. You may be too busy working games to be on the lookout for ways to get better.

The first requisite for improvement is to acknowledge that you are not a polished expert, that some ingrained habits and personal tendencies may be detrimental to your officiating, and that you could benefit from advice for altering your techniques. Superior officials know that there is always more to be learned. The key ingredient in becoming better is to admit your fallibility and seek ways to expand your knowledge.

Advice From Experts

Nearly every official who has risen in the profession is grateful to someone who supplied help at a critical time. Some local associations arrange to have veterans work with newcomers in formal mentoring programs (a successful mentoring program was described in the previous chapter), though such programs may not be well organized or operating when you need them. An official can benefit considerably by seeking the advice of experienced officials on an informal, personal basis. Casual coffee-shop encounters with officials who are widely respected may prove even more beneficial than a formal program. Most highly regarded individuals are flattered to be asked their opinions about tactics. They may also furnish advice on how to move up the ladder to prestigious games and college opportunities.

Working a state high school championship is a special achievement. Nearly every official who has risen in the profession is grateful to someone who supplied help at a critical time.

Even without a formal program, you can consider an informal mentoring arrangement. You might ask an experienced official to observe and comment on a game that you work. The official who is eager to pick up new ideas can also ben-efit by observing a veteran in action and discussing philosophy afterward. An ideal situation is for a learner to work a game or two with a veteran to allow observation and practice of more intricate on-field or on-court approaches.

Self-Assessment

In addition to seeking advice from respected veterans, the official who wants to improve should engage in deliberate self-assessment after each contest. A danger for many officials, as mentioned earlier, is to become self-satisfied, which means not questioning your own judgment and not evaluating the way you dealt with difficult situations. A reasonable way to start a self-assessment is to write down after games which calls seemed to be controversial and how you reacted to objections. Another area for introspection is the way you dealt with coaches and players. If your explanations were unsatisfactory, recall what was said, and mentally develop an alternate way of saying what is appropriate. Refer to chapter 6 on dealing with conflict and chapter 4 on body language and verbal responses; try to recall how you reacted to specific game situations, both ordinary and controversial judgments. Ask yourself the following questions:

▮ Did you resolve conflicts satisfactorily?

▮ Did you anticipate team strategies accurately and in a timely way?

▮ Was your judgment on given plays emphatic and correct?

Veteran Observers

Tom Balle, assignment secretary of the DuPage Valley High School Conference in suburban Chicago, has a cadre of ex-officials that he uses to evaluate the football officials assigned to his conference games. The former officials must notify the game officials of their presence, and then these observers spend the half-time sharing their observations with the crew. An after-game session is optional, depending on the crew's preference, but Balle has reported that observers are almost always asked for a postgame debriefing. He noted that some crews resist being evaluated, especially if they feel that the observer has antiquated notions of how they are supposed to perform, but the " old-timers" themselves feel that their experience helps them to gauge a crew's performance. Instead of retiring to obscurity, the observing veterans gain satisfaction by returning something of value to the sport.

- Did you overlook anything, either elements of play or player behavior?
- Were you influenced by crowd reaction or by verbal attacks from participants?

Another form of review is asking for an honest response from partners or crewmates. Ask those you work with whether any of your habits seem to have negative outcomes. "Is my strike zone consistent? Am I moving into position to make calls correctly? Have I been too loose in calls or too tight? Am I letting the players play the game? Am I intruding too much on play action? Am I calling undue attention to myself?" Those are all legitimate issues and ones that are correctable if you concentrate on improving.

The official who wants to improve should engage in deliberate self-assessment after each contest. That includes weighing factors that may have influenced judgments and also deciding if team strategies were anticipated accurately.

Another way to observe yourself at work is to ask coaches or game administrators for videotapes of games that you have officiated. Nowadays, teams tape many of their games and sometimes even their practice scrimmages. Officials often take blank tapes along and ask game administrators to record the game and return the tapes, which most schools are willing to do. There is perhaps no better way to see how you really look in a game than to view a video of yourself in action.

Clinics

Many camps, clinics, and seminars are available for officials, some arranged by state associations and some set up by colleges, leagues, college commissioners, and private individuals. A few certified camps are conducted each winter by major league baseball umpires before their season starts. *Certified* means that organized professional baseball leagues depend on these camps to supply them with candidates for minor league umpiring.

Football, basketball, baseball, softball, soccer, and volleyball are sports ordinarily served by overnight camps on college campuses. These prolonged clinics often include the opportunity to work games, because they are combined with athletic participation by high school students. If scrimmages and games are part of the experience, videotaping of officials at work is also usually offered, as are personal evaluations by college officials and college commissioners.

Such camps have another value: an opportunity to network with people who can advance your career. Some camps are conducted by the college officiating directors. They use the camps to scout prospective officials for their leagues. Often officials from the college conference are the camp instructors, and they also evaluate prospects if a college commissioner is not present. This is a rich opportunity for learning a great deal about how to officiate at a level higher than you may be working at present. Once again, some of the best information may come your way during off-hours, when officials gather in dormitories or at meals.

Some state organizations sponsor overnight camps, but most of them conduct their clinics on

Attending clinics and camps provides rich opportunities for learning about how to officiate at a level higher than you may be working at present. These educational opportunities also reinforce the fundamentals of solid mechanics.

weekends. Again, these clinics offer the opportunity to meet officials at a higher level, because generally the state associations rely on college officials to impart their advice and philosophies to aspiring officials. State or regional clinics may invite professional officials to deliver presentations, providing valuable information about how officiating takes place at the highest levels of sport. An important dimension of professional officiating is the way officials deal with pressure and handle vast public exposure. Professional officials also have advice to offer about relations with players and coaches. Once more, the opportunity exists for officials to learn from one another in an informal atmosphere. Sharing experiences may be the most noteworthy part of such gatherings.

Studying the Rules

Learning the rules and staying abreast of changes is another important part of growth. Some officials pride themselves on being experts at rule interpretation, while others coast along on perfunctory knowledge. Beyond learning the rules, you must take the important next step: applying the rules in a reasonable way. Rules can be applied to the letter or in a spirit that upholds the primary purposes of the game. All officiating manuals urge that officials apply the spirit of the rules in making judgments. Experience and consultation with other officials will help you understand how to apply the rules in keeping with the spirit of the game.

Superior officials study the rules continually. Often officials set aside a time of day to read a segment of the rule book. It is almost impossible to pore over page after page of rules and retain what you have read, so you should study only a small section of the rule book at a time. Discussion with other officials also is helpful in solidifying the rules in one's mind. This is a major function of some officiating associations; many associations make it a point to feature every single rule on their instructional agenda during the course of a season. Rule books are accompanied

Know the rules, know what to call, and know how to communicate using proper signals—that's the entire essence of working games correctly.

by case books, which are published by the National Federation of State High School Associations and portray game situations in which rules have to be applied in special ways. These texts are useful tools for mastering the intricacies of a sport. When officials get together, they often pose game-situation problems to one another, much as the case books do, as a way of reinforcing their grasp of fine points.

Seeking Opportunities at Other Levels

Officials who want to rise in the profession customarily seek opportunities for exposure beyond their normal operating circles. For instance, if you aspire to work at the college level, it is important to be seen working college scrimmages or off-season practice sessions. Working at different levels provides an official with a broader perspective of how games should be handled. Sometimes this chance to work at more advanced levels may occur at camps or clinics, as previously discussed, but you generally must seek out these opportunities by inquiring when such practices take place and by asking to be involved. To rise above your current level, you must let it be known that you are entertaining such ambitions. The big leagues

will not send someone to scout you unless you tell them that you are interested.

Advancing to the Next Level

The saying "the cream rises to the top" can readily be applied to sports officials. If a person shows exceptional promise, someone above usually notices. However, just as it is the rare athlete who becomes a standout college performer, so too are the opportunities for officials to advance limited, because there are fewer opportunities and the competition for them is keen. But college officials retire, which often makes room for aspiring high school officials to advance. Attending camps, as noted earlier, is one way to open the door to advancement.

Sports officials note as they move to advanced levels that games are played with more intensity, the athletes move more swiftly, they are more skilled, and emotional levels frequently are higher. These factors mean that an official's reactions must be geared to the increased speed and skill and that an official must adjust his or her personal responses to deal effectively with college athletes and coaches. A lot of beneficial experience is necessary to acquire the judgmental skill necessary to handle college sports. Some officials try to move too quickly, and their aspirations are stymied when their abilities don't match their desires.

To officiate at a higher level, you must first know the protocols for entering the collegiate ranks in your geographic region. These protocols vary, but usually you must make a formal application to the commissioner of officials in your sport. A résumé of past experience is usually required, as are recommendations from prominent officials who have either worked directly with you or have seen you in action.

A fact of life is that sometimes advancement depends more on who you know than what you know. Officials who work the conference or college coaches with whom you are acquainted may aid your entry into collegiate ranks. Most college commissioners rely on their own staff and current officials to recommend those who are ready to make the step to a higher level.

College officiating places extreme demands on an official's time. Officials often are required to attend off-season sessions for rules review, training in special tactics, testing, and fitness checks. College games are likely to be far from where you live, making it necessary to set aside more time than you ordinarily would for a high school commitment. You may be required to be at a game site a day in advance, and long hours in an auto or a plane may be necessary to reach a destination out of state.

Although college officials may enjoy a higher status than high school officials, college officials often report an added strain on their family lives and marriages. Strong ambition may be a requisite for high-level officiating. High-level officials must be driven to excel, and such a drive some-

It's nice to be in the big games. There is good news and bad news, however, about moving to higher levels. The prestige and advanced style of competition are gratifying. But the pressure is huge, including substantial time commitments plus intense media scrutiny.

times poses problems for a primary job or family relationships. Upper-level officials admit that an increased paycheck means increased expectations for excellence and less tolerance for error. You can be sure of being evaluated more critically in college than at the high school level. Stress may replace enjoyment for those who do not relish the added pressure.

These are some factors that can inhibit an official's advancement:

- *Arrogance.* An official can be too glib to progress. People who select upper-level officials prefer those who are not know-it-alls.

- *Slow reactions.* At higher levels, instant decisiveness is of utmost importance. A desultory or overly casual style of officiating will work against your being considered for high levels.

- *Stubbornness.* You must show a willingness to learn and improve.

- *Antagonism.* If you consider coaches as enemies and treat them accordingly, you are not likely to advance very far. In contrast, talent as a diplomat is likely to earn you quicker advancement than exceptional game techniques. The same goes for how you treat other crew members. You have to be a team player to rise.

Retaining the Enjoyment

Just as players in the games should have an exhilarating time, so too should officials find their activity satisfying. A prominent baseball official from Arvada, Colorado, named Earl Schoepflin has his crewmates join hands before each game and pledge "to work hard and to have fun." Those two ingredients are essential for a gratifying, long-term officiating career. Athletic competition can be keen and still be enjoyable. Sometimes players show that officials are welcome in their games. They may say, "Good job, ref," or "Nice going, blue," as they leave for their bus or locker room. That's the reward for competence.

The excitement and pleasure of sports exist in the present moment. That is, sports are dramatic; the outcome seems to mean so much when the game is underway. Though the results frequently turn into dim memories, it is the vitality of the present moment, with the outcome unknown, that makes games special. Officials can easily feel part of that urgency and excitement, but the awareness that people consider the game to be more important than it really is can work against an official's enjoyment of the game, too.

Because officials are essential to sports competition, their participation is often satisfying. Officials feel that they are performing a vital service and that they are part of the action. Healthy athletic competition requires outstanding offici-

Reasons for Retiring

Officials who give up working often retire because of other pressing needs in their lives. Sometimes primary career demands usurp the time needed to officiate; officials may want to watch their own children participate in sports; sometimes family activities erode officiating opportunities; sometimes a person develops other interests. Sometimes, however, officials quit the profession due to frustration. Frustration may develop from an inability to advance to desired higher levels, but most often frustration is the result of being underappreciated. Officials must take a lot of heat. "We're expected to be perfect from the start and then get better," one slogan says, and often the public does indeed expect perfection. When evidence of a shortcoming arises, a great deal of unfair criticism is leveled at officials. Such criticism is frequent at higher levels, but high school sports are not immune from biased attacks. This can be discouraging to dedicated officials, and an adversarial atmosphere at games can cause an official to say, "I don't need this," and resign.

Officials are never considered "winners," but they are! They make sure contests are played fairly and by the rules. That truly is winning.

ating. An official should look forward to working a game as much as players anticipate playing it. If officiating becomes a chore or an unpleasant duty, then perhaps the time has come to walk away from it. Sometimes officials burden themselves with too many games or extra commitments besides officiating that can detract from the joy of working games.

Summary

Officiating can continue to be exciting as long as officials stay tuned to the nuances of competi-

tive play and continue to expand their personal horizons. You never can learn all there is to know.

Continual improvement is the key to officiating satisfaction. Learning something from each game is a worthy aim. Officials should stay aware of the many avenues available for improvement and advancement. The inner satisfaction of performing well may be the only recognition an official gets. It is hard to win accolades, but respect from peers and a genuine pleasure in doing a necessary job well can be reward enough. The highest compliment perhaps may come from realizing that someone is using *you* as a role model.

Sports Officials' Code of Ethics

The National Association of Sports Officials (NASO) believes the duty of sports officials is to act as impartial judges of sports competitions. We believe this duty carries with it an obligation to perform with accuracy, fairness, and objectivity through an overriding sense of integrity.

Although the vast majority of sports officials work contests played by amateur athletes, it is vital that every official approach each assignment in a professional manner. Because of their authority and autonomy, officials must have a high degree of commitment and expertise. NASO believes these facts impose on sports officials the higher ethical standard by which true professionals are judged.

Officials who are "professionals" voluntarily observe a high level of conduct, not because they fear a penalty but because of their own personal character. They accept responsibility for their actions. This conduct has as its foundation a deep sense of moral values and use of reason that substantiates the belief a given conduct is proper simply because it is.

The Code

The purposes of the National Association of Sports Officials Code of Ethics are briefly summarized through the following three provisions:

1. To provide our members a meaningful set of guidelines for their professional conduct and to provide them with agreed-upon standards of practice;

2. To provide to other sports officials these same guidelines and standards of practice for their consideration;

3. To provide to others (i.e., players, coaches, administrators, fans, media) criteria by which to judge our actions as "professionals."

NASO has adopted this code and strongly urges its members and officials in general to adhere to its principles. By doing so, notice is given that we recognize the need to preserve and encourage confidence in the professionalism of officiating. This confidence must first be fostered within the "community" of officials and then within the public generally.

NASO believes the integrity of officiating rests on the integrity and ethical conduct of each individual official. This integrity and conduct are the very basis of the future and well-being of organized sports and the effectiveness of this association. NASO shall, by programs of education and other means, encourage acceptance and implementation of the articles named below. To these ends NASO declares acceptance of the following code:

Article I

Sports officials must be free of obligation to any interest other than the impartial and fair judging of sports competitions. Without equivocation, game decisions slanted by personal bias are dishonest and unacceptable.

Article II

Sports officials recognize that anything that may lead to a conflict of interest, either real or apparent, must be avoided. Gifts, favors, special treatment, privileges, employment, or a personal relationship with a school or team that can compromise the perceived impartiality of officiating must be avoided.

Article III

Sports officials are obligated to treat other officials with professional dignity and courtesy and recognize that it is inappropriate to criticize other officials publicly.

Article IV

Sports officials have a responsibility to continuously seek self-improvement through study of the game, rules, mechanics, and the techniques of game management. They have a responsibility to accurately represent their qualifications and abilities when requesting or accepting officiating assignments.

Article V

Sports officials shall protect the public (including fans, administrators, coaches, and players) from inappropriate conduct and shall attempt to eliminate from the officiating avocation/profession all practices that bring discredit to the profession.

Article VI

Sports officials shall not be party to actions designed to unfairly limit or restrain access to officiating, officiating assignments, or association membership. This includes selection for positions of leadership based on economic factors, race, creed, color, age, sex, physical handicap, country, or national origin.

State High School Associations CIF Sections

Alabama High School Athletic Association
926 Pelham Street
Montgomery, AL   36104
334-263-6994
fax 334-240-3389

Alaska School Activities Association
4120 Laurel Street   Suite #102
Anchorage, AK   99508
907-563-3723
fax 907-561-0720

Arizona Interscholastic Association, Inc.
7007 N. 18th St.
Phoenix, AZ   85020-5552
602-385-3810
fax 602-385-3779

Arkansas Activities Association
3920 Richards Rd.
North Little Rock, AR   72117-2233
501-955-2500
fax 501-955-2521

California Interscholastic Federation
664 Las Gallinas
San Rafael, CA   94903
415-492-5911
fax 415-492-5919

Colorado School Activities Association
14855 E. Second Avenue
Aurora, CO   80011
303-344-5050
fax 303-367-4101

Connecticut Interscholastic
Athletic Conference, Inc.
30 Realty Drive
Cheshire, CT   06410
203-250-1111
fax 203-250-1345

Delaware Secondary School
Athletic Association
Federal & Lockerman Streets
John G. Townsend Bldg.
Dover, DE   19901-2899
302-739-4181
fax 302-739-4221

DC Interscholastic Athletic Association
DC Public Schools, Dept. of Athletics
Truesdell School
800 Ingraham Street NW
Washington, DC   20011-2925
202-576-7167
fax 202-576-8505

Florida High School Activities Association
515 N. Main Street
Gainesville, FL   32602-1173
352-372-9551
fax 352-373-1528

Georgia High School Association
151 S. Bethel Street
Thomaston, GA   30286
706-647-7473
fax 706-647-2638

Hawaii High School Athletic Association
P. O. Box 62029
Honolulu, HI 96839
808-587-4495
fax 808-587-4496

Idaho High School Activities Association
8011 Ustick Road
Boise, ID 83704
208-375-7027
fax 208-322-5505

Illinois High School Association
2715 McGraw Drive
Bloomington, IL 61702
309-663-6377
fax 309-663-7479

Indiana High School Athletic Association
9150 N. Meridian Street
Indianapolis, IN 46260
317-846-6601
fax 317-575-4244

Iowa High School Athletic Association
1605 S. Story
Boone, IA 50036
515-432-2011
fax 515-432-2961

Kansas State HS Activities Association, Inc.
520 SW 27th Street
Topeka, KS 66611
785-235-9201
fax 785-235-2637

Kentucky HS Athletic Association
2280 Executive Drive
Lexington, KY 40505-4808
606-299-5472
fax 606-293-5999

Louisiana HS Athletic Association
7905 Wrenwood Blvd.
Baton Rouge, LA 70809
225-925-0100
fax 225-925-5801

Maine Principals' Association
16 Winthrop Street
Augusta, ME 04338
207-622-0217
fax 207-622-1513

Maryland Public Secondary
Schools Athletic Association
200 W. Baltimore Street
Baltimore, MD 21201-1595
410-767-0376
fax 410-333-3111

Massachusetts Interscholastic
Athletic Association, Inc.
83 Cedar Street
Milford, MA 01757
508-478-5641
fax 508-634-3044

Michigan HS Athletic Association
1661 Ramblewood Drive
East Lansing, MI 48823
517-332-5046
fax 517-332-4071

Minnesota State HS League
2100 Freeway Blvd.
Brooklyn Center, MN 55430-1735
612-560-2262
fax 612-569-0499

Mississippi HS Activities Association
1201 Clinton-Raymond Road
Clinton, MS 39060-0244
601-924-6400
fax 601-924-1725

Missouri State HS Activities Association
1808 Interstate 70 Drive SW
Columbia, MO 65205-1328
573-445-4443
fax 573-445-2502

Montana HS Association
1 South Dakota Avenue
Helena, MT 59601-5198
406-442-6010
fax 406-442-8250

Nebraska School Activities Association
8230 Beechwood Drive
Lincoln, NE 68505-0447
402-489-0386
fax 402-489-0934

Nevada Interscholastic
Activities Association
1 East Liberty Street Suite #505
Reno, NV 89501
775-688-6464
fax 775-688-6466

New Hampshire Interscholastic
Athletic Association, Inc.
251 Clinton Street
Concord, NH   03301-0384
603-228-8671
fax 603-225-7978

New Jersey State Interscholastic
Athletic Association
P. O. Box 487
Robbinsville, NJ 08691
609-259-2776
fax 609-259-3047

New Mexico Activities Association
6600 Palomas NE
Albuquerque, NM   87109
505-821-1887
fax 505-821-2441

New York State Public
HS Athletic Association, Inc.
88 Delaware Avenue
Delmar, NY   12054-1599
518-439-8872
fax 518-475-1556

North Carolina HS
Athletic Association, Inc.
P. O. Box 3216
Chapel Hill, NC   27515-3216
919-962-2345
fax 919-962-1686

North Dakota HS
Activities Association
134 NE Third Street
Valley City, ND   58072
701-845-3953
fax 701-845-4935

Ohio HS Athletic Association
4080 Roselea Place
Columbus, OH   43214-3070
614-267-2502
fax 614-267-1677

Oklahoma Secondary School
Activities Association
7300 N. Broadway Extension
Oklahoma City, OK   73116-9012
405-840-1116
fax 405-840-9559

Oregon School Activities Association
25200 SW Parkway Avenue, Suite #1
Wilsonville, OR   97070
503-682-6722
fax 503-682-0960

Pennsylvania Interscholastic
Athletic Association, Inc.
550 Gettysburg Road
Mechanicsburg, PA   17055
717-697-0374
fax 717-697-7721

Rhode Island Interscholastic
League, Inc.
Bldg. #6   R.I. College Campus
600 Mt. Pleasant Avenue
Providence, RI   02908-1991
401-272-9844
fax 401-272-9838

South Carolina HS League
121 Westpark Blvd.
Columbia, SC   29210
803-798-0120
fax 803-731-9679

South Dakota HS Activities Association
204 N. Euclid
Pierre, SD   57501
605-224-9261
fax 605-224-9262

Tennessee Secondary School
Athletic Association
3333 Lebanon Road
Hermitage, TN   37076
615-889-6740
fax 615-889-0544

Texas University
Interscholastic League
1701 Manor Road
Austin, TX   78722
512-471-5883
fax 512-471-6589

Utah HS Activities Association
199 East 7200 South
Midvale, UT   84047
801-566-0681
fax 801-566-0633

Vermont Principals' Association, Inc.
Two Prospect Street, Suite #3
Montpelier, VT   05602
802-229-0547
fax 802-229-4801

Virginia HS League
1642 State Farm Blvd.
Charlottesville, VA   22911-8809
804-977-8475
fax 804-977-5943

Washington Interscholastic
Activities Association
435 Main Ave.
South, Renton, WA   98055
425-687-8585
fax 425-687-9476

West Virginia Secondary School
Activities Commission
Route 9 Box 76
Parkersburg, WV   26101-9158
304-485-5494
fax 304-428-5431

Wisconsin Interscholastic
Athletic Association
5516 Vern Holmes Dr.
Stevens Point, WI   54481
715-344-8580
fax 715-344-4241

Wyoming HS Activities Association
731 E. 2nd Street
Casper, WY   82601-2620
307-577-0614
fax 307-577-0637

CIF – Central Section
2555 Clovis Avenue
Clovis, CA   93612
559-292-7580
fax 559-202-3838

CIF – Central Coast Section
1691 Old Bayshore Hwy.
Suite #200
San Jose, CA   95112
408-441-9505
fax 408-441-9509

CIF – Los Angeles City Section
716 E. 14th Street
Bungalow #AA-453
Los Angeles, CA   90021
213-743-3640
fax 213-746-6390

CIF – North Coast Section
8151 Village Parkway Bldg. C-1
Dublin, CA   94568
925-828-4900
fax 925-828-5700

CIF – Northern Section
895 Hale Ave., P.O. Box 40
Arbuckle, CA   95912
530-476-3830
fax 530-476-3831

CIF – Oakland Section
Oakland City Schools
1025 Second Avenue
Oakland, CA   94606
510-879-8311
fax 510-879-1835

CIF – San Diego Section
6401 Linda Vista Road   Room 404
San Diego, CA   92111-7399
619-292-8165
fax 619-292-1375

CIF – San Francisco Section
300 Seneca Avenue   Room #2
San Francisco, CA   94112
415-452-4932
fax 415-452-4935

CIF – San Joaquin Section
2405 S. Stockton Street   #2
Lodi, CA   95240
209-334-5900
fax 209-334-0300

CIF – Southern Section
11011 E. Artesia Blvd.
Cerritos, CA   90703
562-860-2414
fax 562-860-1692

Other Governing Bodies

Amateur Baseball Umpires Association
(ABUA)
572 Oak Valley
Frontenac, MO   63131

American Youth Soccer Organization
(AYSO)
12501 South Isis Avenue
Hawthorne, CA   90250
800/872-2976
fax 310/643-5310

Arena Football League (AFL)
75 E. Wacker   #1000
Chicago, IL   60601
312/332-5510

Babe Ruth League, Inc.
1770 Brunswick Pike
Trenton, NJ   08638
609/695-1434

Continental Basketball Association (CBA)
Two Arizona Center
400 N. 5th St.   #1425
Phoenix, AZ   85004
602/254-6677

Little League Baseball, Inc.
P.O. Box 3485
Williamsport, PA   17701
570/326-1921

National Alliance for Youth Sports
2050 Vista Parkway
West Palm Beach, FL   33411
561/684-1141

National Association for Girls and
Women in Sports (NAGWS)
1900 Association Drive
Reston, VA   22091
703/476-3452

National Association of
Intercollegiate Athletics (NAIA)
6120 South Yale Avenue #1450
Tulsa, OK   74136
918/494-8828

National Association of Sports Officials (NASO)
2017 Lathrop Avenue
Racine, WI   53405
262/632-8855
fax 262/632-5460

National Basketball Association (NBA)
Olympic Tower
645 Fifth Avenue
New York, NY   10022
212/407-8000

National Collegiate Athletic Association (NCAA)
700 W. Washington St.
1 NCAA Plaza
Indianapolis, IN 46204
317/917-6222

National Federation of State HS Associations
690 W. Washington
Indianapolis, IN 46204
317/972-6900

National Football League (NFL)
280 Park Avenue
New York, NY   10017
212/450-2000

National Intercollegiate Soccer
Officials Association (NISOA)
541 Woodview Drive
Longwood, FL   32779
407/862-3305

National Junior College
Athletic Association (NJCAA)
P.O. Box 7305
Colorado Springs, CO   80933-7305
719/590-9788

Pony Baseball & Softball
P.O. Box 225
Washington, PA   15301
412/225-1060

Pop Warner Football
586 Middletown Blvd. Suite C-100
Langhorne, PA   19047
215/752-2691

Soccer Association For Youth (SAY)
4050 Executive Park Drive Suite #100
Cincinnati, OH   45241
800/233-7291
513/769-0500

Soccer in the Streets (SITS)
149 S. McDonough Street   Suite 270
Jonesboro, GA   30236
770/477-0354
770/478-1862

USA Hockey
1775 Bob Johnson Drive
Colorado Springs, CO   80906

USA Volleyball
One Olympic Plaza
Colorado Springs, CO   80910
719/637-8300

United States Olympic Committee
One Olympic Plaza
Colorado Springs, CO   80909

United States Soccer Federation
(USSF)
1801-1811 South Prairie Avenue
Chicago, IL   60616
312/808-1300
fax 312/808-1301

Women's National Basketball Association
(WNBA)
Olympic Tower
645 Fifth Avenue
New York, NY   10022
212/688-9622

Index

About the Editor

Jerry Grunska

Referee is the premier magazine for sports officiating. It began publication in 1976 and is recognized as the leading authority and voice for officials at all levels of sports. The publisher of *Referee*, Barry Mano was the driving force in the founding of the National association of Sports Officials (NASO) and is a leading spokesperson for officials throught the country. *Referee* is headquartered in Racine, Wisconsin.

Jerry Grunska serves as editor of *Successful Sports Officiating* and has over forty years of officiating experience at the high school and college levels. He has coauthored several books on officiating, including *The Officials Guide: Football, Take Charge Football Officiating*, and *Better Football Officiating*. He also frequently writes articles for Referee. In addition to Grunska, the following experts in the field of officiating contributed to *Successful Sports Officiating:* **Mel Narol** is a partner with the Princeton, New Jersey law firm of Pellettieri, Rabstein and Altman. He is the foremost authority on sports officials and the law and has published more than 150 articles and is a frequent lecturer on the subject. He was an active basketball referee and has been a law columnist for *Referee Magazine* since 1981. **Kathleen Poole, PhD** is the health promotion coordinator at Virginia Tech University. She is a well-known speaker on health-related issues and has been widely published in the field. **John Poole, EdD** is assistant professor of health and physical education at Virginia Tech University. He has written authoritatively in the field of personal fitness, training and health. **Kay Roof-Steffen, MA** is an instructor at Muscatine Community College, Muscatine, Iowa. She is an accomplished and respected freelance writer in the fields of health, recreation and physical fitness. **George A. Selleck, PhD** is a psychologist turned business and sports consultant and a former basketball star at Stanford University. He has written books on the subject of success in sports and in life and gives workshops designed to help athletes become winners in life. **Doug Toole** is a physical therapist and was primarily responsible for the development of the training regimen for the officials in the National Football League. He has been an official in the NFL since 1988. **Bill Topp** is editor of *Referee Magazine* and has been on the magazine's staff since 1990. He umpires baseball at the NCAA Division I level and officiates basketball and football at the NCAA Division III and high school levels. He is a frequent seminar presenter to officiating groups. **Henry A. Zaborniak, Jr.** is an assistant commissioner with the Ohio High School Athletic Association. He is a former high school coach and is an active football official in the Big Ten Collegiate Conference.

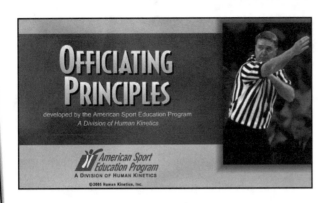

The OFFICIATING PRINCIPLES online course can help you be a better official this season!

Officiating Principles is a sport-neutral online course offering officials of all sports the baseline knowledge to officiate games with confidence and poise.

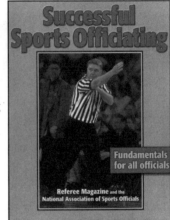

After registering for the course, you'll be sent a personal copy of the 175-page book *Successful Sports Officiating*, which you'll use while taking the online course, providing for an engaging interactive experience.

After completing the course, the book is yours to keep for referring to throughout the season and for years to come.

Course participants take the test online and receive immediate results. Those who pass are entered into the National Officials Registry (NOR), a database of officials accessible by anyone looking for qualified officials. Inclusion in the NOR provides officials added credibility and visibility.

OFFICIATING PRINCIPLES ONLINE COURSE

American Sport Education Program
(A Division of Human Kinetics)
ISBN: 978-0-7360-7860-3
Price: $75.00
Price includes: One-year access to the online course, the *Successful Sports Officiating* book, and inclusion in the National Officials Registry.

Ideal for those just entering the officiating ranks or for those looking for a refresher in the basics. The course covers these topics:

- Determining your officiating philosophy and your officiating style
- Setting and achieving professional goals
- Communicating effectively with other officials, coaches, and athletes
- Developing your decision-making skills and managing conflict
- Explaining the principles of personal fitness and creating a personal fitness plan
- Identifying your legal responsibilities, legal rights, and business responsibilities
- Managing your time wisely
- Working with local and regional associations
- Managing your officiating career

With *the Officiating Principles* online course, you'll be prepared, confident, and motivated to officiate high school contests and manage your officiating career. Register today! Visit the course catalog at www.ASEP.com or call 800-747-5698.

A DIVISION OF HUMAN KINETICS